FORTS OF THE AMERICAN REVOLUTION 1775–83

RENÉ CHARTRAND   ILLUSTRATED BY DONATO SPEDALIERE

Series Editor Marcus Cowper

First published in Great Britain in 2016 by Osprey Publishing,
PO Box 883, Oxford, OX1 9PL, UK
1385 Broadway, 5th Floor, New York, NY 10018, USA
E-mail: info@ospreypublishing.com

A CIP catalog record for this book is available from the British Library.

ISBN: 978 1 4728 1445 6
PDF e-book ISBN: 978 1 4728 1446 3
e-Pub ISBN: 978 1 4728 1447 0

Editorial by Ilios Publishing Ltd, Oxford, UK (www.iliospublishing.com)
Index by Fionbar Lyons
Typeset in Myriad Pro and Sabon
Maps by Bounford.com
Artwork illustrations by Donato Spedaliere
Originated by PDQ Media, Bungay, UK
Printed in China through World Print Ltd.

16 17 18 19 20 10 9 8 7 6 5 4 3 2 1

ARTIST'S NOTE

Readers may care to note that the original paintings from which the color
plates in this book were prepared are available for private sale. The
Publishers retain all reproduction copyright whatsoever. The artist can
be contacted via the following email address:
alina@alinaillustrazioni.com
The Publishers regret that they can enter into no correspondence upon
this matter.

AUTHOR'S NOTE

It can be said that the subject of this study is very fleeting because the
fortifications were, except for Quebec City, nearly all temporary earth
and wooden structures that were often quickly put together to meet
an immediate purpose. They were numerous, came in all sizes and shapes,
and appeared and disappeared all over eastern North America according
to the movements of armies. As a result of this fluidity as well as the
necessarily modest size of this book, a narrative of the main operations
as well as some, but not all, secondary engagements involving the use
of fortifications was chosen as the best way to obtain an overall view.
What emerges is the remarkably important influence the use
of fortifications did have in the struggle and winning of American
independence, typified by the 1781 sieges of Pensacola and Yorktown
that basically ended active operations in North America. A few notes
on the corps of engineers involved and a glossary round out this study.
The author wishes to thank and laud editors Marcus Cowper and Nikolai
Bogdanovic and the illustrators for their great work and patience in dealing
with the rather complicated aspects of this very diverse and fascinating
subject. He also particularly thanks the Library of Congress, the Boston
Public Library, the Yale University Art Gallery, and the Anne S. K. Brown
Collection at the Brown University Library for their remarkable online
access in high resolution to superlative maps and plans, the few
reproduced in this study being a minute fraction of the impressive
collections presented in the true and free spirit of the dissemination
of knowledge to all.

THE WOODLAND TRUST

Osprey Publishing are supporting the Woodland Trust, the UK's leading
woodland conservation charity, by funding the dedication of trees.

CONTENTS

FORTS OF THE AMERICAN REVOLUTION 1775–83

INTRODUCTION

Although the American War of Independence was largely fought in the field, it could also be said that many of the key battles of the conflict were sieges against fortified positions. Some of these engagements were large-scale affairs, worthy of any siege in Europe; indeed, Yorktown, the most important siege in the American theater of operations, had such an impact that the town's surrender led to Great Britain losing the war. However, there were hardly any fortified cities or large stone citadels in North America. Most cities only had a few batteries and no effective curtain walls to enclose them.

The military engineers of four nations were active in the 1775–83 North American campaigns. All sides resorted to constructing a wide variety of earthen and wooden field fortifications according to the various European military engineering manuals, all of them inspired by the principles of French Marshal Sébastien Le Prestre de Vauban (1633–1707), arguably one of history's greatest military engineers.

Key fortifications from the American Revolutionary War

At the outset of the war, the British Army's Corps of Engineers was responsible for protecting Great Britain's possessions in North America, but initially very few commissioned professional engineers were present. In 1775, out of 61 engineer officers in the corps, there was only one in Quebec, one in Montreal, one in Halifax, one in Boston, one in New York, and one at Pensacola. During the conflict, the number of officers, who served with competence and distinction in North America, rose to 38, although they were too few: the whole corps only numbered 75 engineers in 1780. Aspiring British engineers usually attended the Royal Military Academy at Woolwich, which mostly educated artillery officers, both services being under the Board of Ordnance and not the "Army" at large in the peculiar organization of Britain's armed forces. Engineers were thus more seen as uniformed technicians rather than fighting officers. It might be added that, due to social class perceptions, they had less influence as general staff officers than engineers in the French, American, or Spanish armies. Be that as it may, those posted to North America during the conflict were overwhelmed with work. For instance, John Montresor was the only engineer officer with General Thomas Gage's army in Boston for most of 1775, a situation often repeated on many occasions during the war.

The Americans did not have a professional establishment of military engineers at the outset of the conflict, although the absolute necessity of having such professionals in their nascent army was recognized. A few

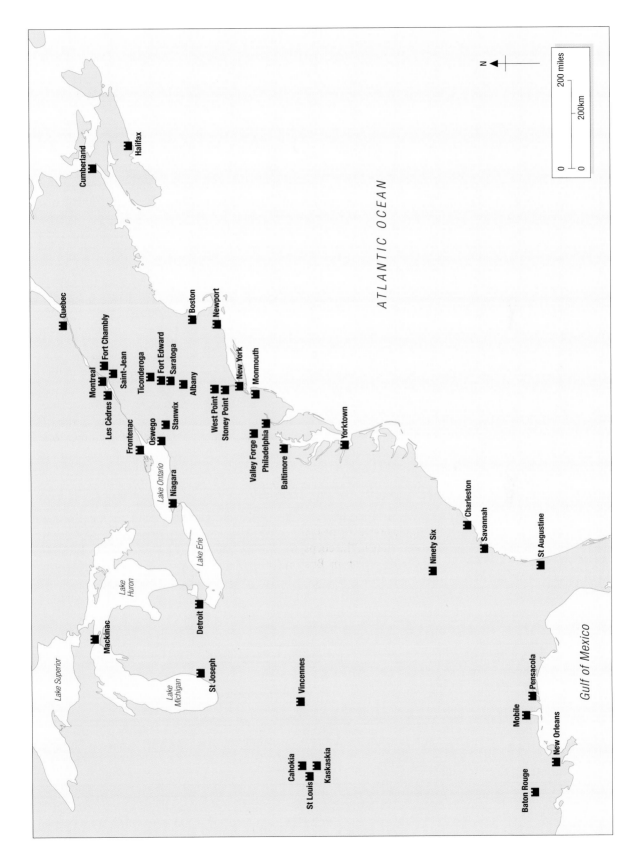

N

200 miles
200km

ATLANTIC OCEAN

Gulf of Mexico

Lake Superior
Lake Huron
Lake Michigan
Lake Erie
Lake Ontario

Halifax
Cumberland
Quebec
Fort Chambly
Montreal
Saint-Jean
Les Cèdres
Ticonderoga
Fort Edward
Saratoga
Frontenac
Stanwix
Oswego
Albany
Boston
Newport
New York
Monmouth
West Point
Stoney Point
Niagara
Valley Forge
Philadelphia
Baltimore
Yorktown
Charleston
Ninety Six
Savannah
St Augustine
Detroit
Mackinac
St Joseph
Vincennes
Cahokia
St Louis
Kaskaskia
Mobile
Pensacola
Baton Rouge
New Orleans

5

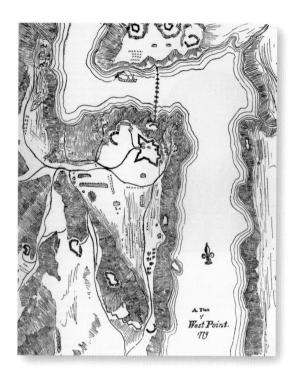

The main works at West Point according to a map of 1779 – a print after a drawing by Moses Greenleaf. The main works of forts Clinton (upper center) and Putnam (lower left) were the main citadels protecting the American army's main supply base. West Point also had numerous outer redoubts on both sides of the Hudson River that made the place nearly impregnable. (Private collection; author's photograph)

Americans had gleaned some engineering knowledge from books and Richard Gridley, William Burbeck, Jeduthan Baldwin, and Rufus Putnam became occasional or permanent engineers serving with General George Washington, but none had been trained at a military academy and all lacked the advanced, specialist skills required of army engineers. European volunteers that had such training were sought and commissioned as engineers in the Continental Army. Some of the early engineer volunteers presenting themselves in 1776 proved to be frauds, while others, notably Polish-born Tadeusz Kosciuszko, would become amongst the most trusted members of the American Corps of Engineers. Nearly all came from France, some "loaned" by the French Army's engineer corps (Corps Royal du Génie) in 1777. One of these was the outstanding Louis Duportail whose obvious expertise, cooperative attitude, and shrewdness led the Americans to appoint him the senior engineer officer with the rank of brigadier-general in November 1777; he is also remembered as the "father of American engineering." A professional American Army engineering branch thus took form. Its initial members were mostly French-trained officers who could contribute the necessary expertise to American armies in the field. While at Valley Forge, Duportail created a modest engineering school later moved to West Point. From 1779, there were three engineer companies of sappers and miners to better supervise the construction of field fortifications. By the later stages of the war, the Americans had developed a military engineering capacity such as never seen before in the country.

From the mid-17th to the mid-19th centuries, French military engineering was considered the most advanced anywhere; not only was it technically excellent, but it also produced the theories and concepts that were often followed by other European powers. This extraordinary influence was largely

A view of West Point, "as it appeared during the Revolution," an engraving from the *New York Magazine* (1790) as per J. W. Barber and H. Howe's *Historical Collections…* (1845). This view is taken from the northeast. A: Constitution Island, on the east side of the Hudson River. B: a chain, 450 yards in length, reaching across the Hudson River. C: Fort Clinton, the main fort situated on the west side of the river and intended to defend West Point against any naval force. (Author's collection)

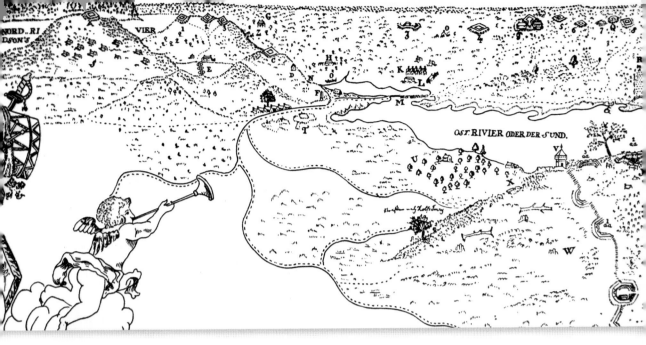

due to the remarkable works created by Marshal Vauban. The École Royale du Génie (Royal Engineering School) at Mézières was considered to offer the world's best engineering education; the latter would prove very useful to the nascent American Corps of Engineers. At the time of the war, the Corps Royal du Génie had an establishment of 329 officers of whom about 25 were posted overseas, mostly in the West Indies. Several more were attached to the Continental Army. For instance, General Jean Rochambeau's French Army serving in the United States was led by Colonel Jean-Nicolas Desandrouins, a veteran of the Canadian campaigns with General Louis-Joseph de Montcalm, and included 11 officers assisting him at the siege of Yorktown. From 1777, the French Army also had a small establishment of specialized *ingénieurs géographes* (topographical engineers) numbering 27 officers. A few colonial engineers also served in the West Indies, mainly looking after the fortifications there; the latter were incorporated into the Corps Royal du Génie after the war.

The Spanish Army's Cuerpo de Ingenieros (Corps of Engineers) was organized in 1711 and closely mirrored the French Army's engineer establishment. Its officers had to graduate from the Real Academia Militar de Matemáticas (Royal Military Academy of Mathematics) in Barcelona, renowned for being an excellent institution. In 1776, the corps had 150 engineer officers, some of whom served in Spain's extensive overseas territories. In North America, this included the vast but sparsely settled territory of Louisiana; engineers were posted to New Orleans for service there. Spanish engineers, and especially those posted overseas, were more concerned with masonry fortifications protecting towns and harbors. In the 1760s, they had expanded the fortifications systems at Havana and San Juan (Puerto Rico), making them the most extensive in the Americas and all but impregnable. Even their lesser forts, notably the North American frontier's "Presidios" that were made of adobe and stone, provided formidable defences against any local enemy threats. The use of field artillery was of secondary consideration, although the capacity to use this was inherent, provided that sufficient time was given to adapt for its use. During the American War of Independence, it was siege artillery largely brought from Havana that proved decisive at the 1781 siege of Pensacola.

The northern sector of Manhattan Island, May 1779, in a print after Von Kraft in Bolton's *Relics of the Revolution*. From 1776, the northern end of Manhattan (at left) and the heights bordering the eastern shore of the East River had many earth and timber works erected by the Americans. They were later occupied by the British, who built several more and then demolished all of them in the autumn of 1779 when they retreated to the fortification line of "circumvallation" (lower right built across Manhattan to deny access further south). (Author's collection)

The engineer corps of France, Britain, and Spain formed the elite of the technical services in their respective armies and comprised highly educated officers who pursued excellence in their fields. They often worked with artillery officers, the other "intellectuals" in those armies, for the maximum efficiency of their respective arts. It was therefore no accident to find many engineer and artillery officers acting as staff officers, particularly in the post-1763 French Army, which had found that effective work by a group of highly educated and trained general staff officers attached to talented generals was a factor influencing a victorious outcome. Of the above-named nations, the French Army (the largest in Europe at the time) probably had the most advanced engineering and staff procedures, some aspects of which were adopted by the Americans, whose practices otherwise reflected the basic concepts and experiences of the colonial militia.

CHRONOLOGY

1775

May	The capture of Fort Ticonderoga by American patriots.
June	The British in Boston are blockaded by American forces.
June 17	The battle of Breed's (or Bunker) Hill.
September	American invasion of Canada.
December	The siege of Quebec begins.

1776

March	The British evacuate Boston.
June	The siege of Charleston. Americans evacuate Canada.
July 4	The American Declaration of Independence is adopted by the Continental Congress meeting at Philadelphia, Pennsylvania.
Aug–Sept	The British occupy New York City.
November	The American invasion of Nova Scotia is repulsed at Fort Cumberland.

1777

August	The siege of Fort Stanwix.
October	The British Army capitulates at Saratoga.
December	The Continental Army winters at Valley Forge.

1778

January	Americans establish a stronghold at West Point.
February	France signs a treaty of friendship with the United States.
July	France declares war on Great Britain.

1779

June	Spain declares war on Great Britain.
July	The Americans capture Stoney Point.
September	Baton Rouge falls to the Spanish.
Sept–Oct	The French and American attack on Savannah is repulsed by the British.

1780

March	Mobile falls to the Spanish.
May	Charleston falls to British forces.
July	The French Army expeditionary corps lands at Newport, Rhode Island.

1781

May	Pensacola surrenders to Spanish forces.
October	The surrender of British troops at Yorktown to American and French forces.

1782

June	The British evacuate Savannah.
November	A preliminary peace agreement is signed.
December	The British evacuate Charleston.

1783

September	The Treaty of Paris ends the war.
November	The British evacuate New York City.

THE NORTHEAST

Boston

On April 19, 1775, a force of 800 British infantrymen marched out of Boston to search and seize arms and ammunition at Concord 20 miles distant which had been gathered there by the "Minutemen" of the Massachusetts Militia. When they arrived at Lexington, Captain John Parker's company of Minutemen blocked the way. No one is sure who fired "the shot heard around the world" on Lexington Green, but the British regulars soon scattered the American militiamen and arrived in Concord only to learn that the arms and ammunition had been hidden away. They also now became increasingly concerned by the presence of thousands of angry American militiamen gathering, who from the cover of trees, bluffs, and fences, began firing at them. The British troops turned back and by the time they reached Boston, 73 soldiers had been killed and 174 wounded. The Americans had lost 49 killed and 41 wounded. The decade-long political crisis between the 13 colonies and the mother country had evolved into war, one that would last for eight years.

The American militiamen from the countryside surrounding Boston took up arms, mobilized for active service, and started digging trenches and building redoubts on the outskirts of the town so as to contain the British troops in the city. The Americans had few artillery pieces and were, in any event, reluctant to fire upon Boston and risk killing their own civilians. Up to that time, Boston had no fortifications save those to repel an attack from a seaborne enemy. The most important was Castle Williams on an island at the harbor's entrance. The British secured Boston Neck, the sole overland access to the city, with three lines of entrenchments that faced the American "circumvallation" trenches just beyond Roxbury. The main British work in the city was a large earthen redoubt built on the summit of Beacon Hill. British reinforcements

American and British fortifications and camps in and around Boston, 1775–76. The Americans built redoubts and defense lines mainly along the northwest and outside Roxbury near Boston Neck (at the bottom of this plan). The city (then occupied by the British) was sited on a peninsula accessible by Boston Neck that was protected by three lines of fortifications with a redoubt and batteries. Other redoubts were built on the western side, where most of the British troops were encamped. The older Fort Hill and the North Battery on the east side were meant to cover the harbor. This detail is from *A Plan of the Town of Boston and its Environs…* by Thomas Hyde Page, Royal Engineers. (Courtesy Library of Congress, Washington)

under generals Henry Clinton, John Burgoyne, and William Howe arrived in May bolstering the commander-in-chief General Thomas Gage's forces to about 10,000 regulars in the city.

By June, some 16,000 American patriot militiamen under Major-General Artemas Ward, the elderly commander of the Massachusetts Militia, were assembled outside Boston and were busy constructing field fortifications and redoubts at various spots to form a perimeter that would block any further British attempts to leave the city. An observer later reported:

> lines of both [Roxbury and Cambridge] are impregnable; with forts (many of which are bombproof) and redoubts, supposing them to be all in a direction, are about twenty miles; the breastworks are of a proper height, and in many places seventeen feet in thickness; the trenches wide and deep in proportion, before which lay forked impediments; and many of the forts, in every respect, are perfectly ready for battle. The whole, in a word, the admiration of every spectator; for verily their fortifications appear to be the works of seven years, instead of about as many months.

For General Gage, it was important to secure the neighboring hills, especially those of Charlestown to the north and of Dorchester to the southeast. Dorchester was somewhat isolated and would require either traversing the American lines and redoubts at Roxbury, then turning east, or crossing by boat; both ways were likely to be difficult, with the added risk of being outflanked by numerous American reinforcements. By contrast, Charlestown was easily accessible by boat from Boston and, up to the evening of June 16, its heights were not occupied by the Americans. On the morning of June 17, General Gage and his officers observed considerable construction activity on Bunker Hill and Breed's Hill, just behind Charlestown, which was situated on a peninsula accessible by the narrow Charlestown Neck between Mill Pound and the Mystic River. It was decided to clear the "Rebels" out of that peninsula and secure Bunker Hill and especially Breed's Hill, where a substantial redoubt was being built.

The American army outside Boston did not have specialized corps such as military engineers, but it did have experienced and knowledgable individuals in elements of artillery, which encompassed many aspects of engineering. The most famous example was the Boston bookseller John Knox, acknowledged ordnance expert on account of his wide reading in the subject, who became the chief gunner in the Continental Army. Some of the older Massachusetts Militia officers had also seen active service during the Seven Years War; the art of digging trenches and erecting redoubts was therefore familiar to them. The above factors explain why the field fortifications built on the outskirts of Boston clearly assumed professional designs such as those found in military manuals. The Americans also knew the main weakness of their force: it could only fight behind cover in a fortified position, given that it was a gathering of militiamen, not of a professional army drilled for months in the intricacies of battalion movements to march in perfect lines under enemy fire as practiced by European armies. It was thus important for the Americans to be familiar with the basics of fortification, and they were.

To secure the Charlestown peninsula area, Gage gathered a force of 3,000 men. Everyone in the British contingent was highly optimistic and it was practically taken for granted that the mob of "rebel peasants" would soon be scattered by infantry and naval bombardments. It was a case of gross overconfidence, however. North-American farmers were different to their European counterparts in that most owned their farms and, in line with colonial militia laws, were required to own muskets that many of them used for hunting – some being quite skilled at target shooting. Unlike the European "peasantry," a substantial proportion of American men were armed and familiar with the basics of military organization as enrolled militiamen. In spite of the previous retreat from Lexington and the fact that hordes of armed Americans blockaded the city and built many field fortifications, the British officers do not seem to have taken the above factors fully into account.

Breed's Hill and Bunker Hill

General Gage could have easily cut off the 2,000 men laboring on the hills of the peninsula by seizing Charlestown Neck. The Americans were intent on

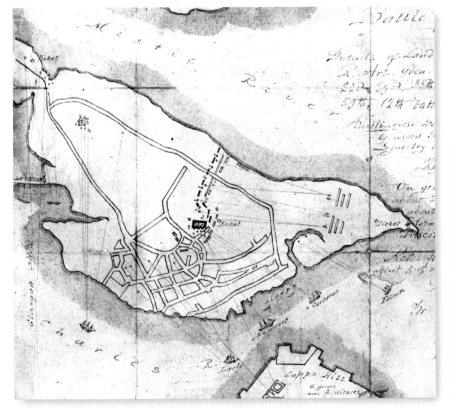

"Plan of the Battle of Bunker Hill," which occurred on June 17, 1775. This plan is especially interesting since it was signed by Major-General Henry Clinton and dated October 4, 1775 as an addition to his earlier report of June 18 on the battle. It is thus probably one of the most accurate showing the event. It shows the large American redoubt on Breed's Hill and the trench line from this to the Mystic River bombarded and attacked by British troops. Also shown at left is the starshaped American redoubt on Bunker Hill being bombarded by British ships. (Courtesy Library of Congress, Washington)

building a large redoubt on Bunker Hill to the north, near the Neck, so as to provide some protection to this access route, but that instruction was misunderstood and most efforts went into fortifying Breed's Hill instead. The earth redoubt was about 40 yards square with 6ft-high parapets mounted with wooden gun platforms; "In the only side on which it could be attacked were two pieces of cannon. In the two salient angles were two trees, with their branches projecting off the parapet, to prevent an entry being made on the angles" (*Gentlemen's Magazine*). Also constructed was a defensive line of earth and stone with a two-rail wooden fence on top complimented by three flèches, running between the Breed's Hill Redoubt and the Mystic River, to cover their left flank. By early afternoon of June 17, the British infantry had landed on the southern end of the peninsula and were forming battle lines. Gage had made the decision simply to attack the American positions at Breed's Hill and along the rail-fence line. In all likelihood, according to Gage, the Americans would break and run away at the sight of the approaching troops; Lexington would be avenged and the rebellion crushed in a matter of hours.

The British line advanced in perfect order simultaneously against the redoubt and the rail-fence. Instead of fleeing, the Americans kept their cool and waited until the British were about 50 yards away. Then they fired a tremendous volley; the whole front rank of British soldiers was hit and went down. Their comrades returned an ineffective fire against the entrenched Americans and, after a few minutes of further casualties, they broke ranks and ran down the hill. The astounded British commanders paused and rallied their men while the exultant Americans cheered. At this time, fire broke out in Charlestown following the bombardment of British ships, and rapidly spread; some 400 buildings were destroyed. The reason for Charlestown's destruction may have been to create a smoke screen for a separate attack, but it did not succeed since a light breeze drove the smoke away from the American entrenchments. At length, a second assault was attempted. Again, the battalions marched up the hill, again the American volleys decimated their ranks; after a short struggle, the British troops retreated once more in disorder, leaving the slopes covered with dead and wounded red-coated soldiers. British casualties were high, while those of the well-protected Americans were, thus far, minimal.

 THE BRITISH ASSAULT ON BREED'S HILL, JUNE 17, 1775

As explained in the main text, the "Battle of Bunker Hill" was fought at Breed's Hill. Due to some confusion, the redoubt built by the Americans during the night of June 16/17 was actually erected on Breed's Hill, a lower eminence of Bunker Hill, and its artillery emplacements were protected by 6ft-high works. Later reports spoke of Bunker Hill and the battle is remembered and commemorated by that name. It has been suggested that gabions were used in these works, but artist John Trumbull watched the battle from the opposite side of the harbor and, in the many paintings of the battle that he made over the next four decades, simply showed mostly earthen works that would have been reinforced with timber although not always visible. Gabions might have been used in limited quantity, but one has to wonder if any would have been made by American patriot militiamen, who were then basically still armed civilians, as early as June 1775. On the night of June 16/17, just getting earth walls up before dawn was the priority and there was certainly no time for the Americans to revet the works with grass or boards. Thus, the earth and pebble appearance given by Trumbull is surely what he saw from afar. At Breed's Hill, the redoubt could give enough cover for the patriots lining the walls to offer good protection while shooting on the advancing ranks of British soldiers. This is the moment shown. It was only when the Americans ran out of ammunition that the British troops at last succeeded in taking the American works. British casualties were very high, proof that Americans could stubbornly hold a simple and hastily built field fortification and wreak havoc.

The British assault on Breed's Hill, June 17, 1775. This 1786 painting is one of Trumbull's early versions. Some of the men shown were actual likenesses. The fatally wounded American Dr Joseph Warren, lying on the ground, is saved by Major Small from being bayoneted by a grenadier while stepping over the fallen Colonel James Abercrombie. The wounded Major John Pitcairn of the Marines, behind Small, is being taken away. American General Israel Putnam is at the far right. British generals William Howe (wearing a hat) and Henry Clinton are brandishing swords in the background near their flag. (Courtesy Yale University Art Gallery, New London, CT)

However, the defenders of Breed's Hill and the rail-fence were running out of ammunition. Furthermore, all was confusion in Major-General Ward's American command further away; the lack of experience in staff work meant that reinforcements and a resupply of ammunition were not forthcoming. At about 5.00pm, the British troops began marching up the hill for a third assault. The Americans fired again and the advancing British columns were shaken, but the defenders' shooting now became more sporadic as they ran out of powder. Seeing this, the British soldiers charged and at last managed to enter the Breed's Hill Redoubt and overcome the fence-rail. Their bayonets slaughtered many Americans, but the latter managed an orderly retreat across Charlestown Neck while the British occupied the other redoubt on Bunker Hill and did not dare go further than the peninsula. It had been a bloody fight by any standard: the British had 1,054 killed and wounded (one soldier in every three deployed, and one in every two engaged), while the Americans had suffered 449 casualties, mostly during the last assault (around a quarter of their force). The British held the ground, but it can be seen as more of an American victory. The "rebels" proved to be brave and resilient fighters when sheltered by good field fortifications which were erected with remarkable speed. Such works could be built quickly and almost anywhere, and the battle of Bunker Hill, as this engagement became known, showed that the American troops could defend their fortified positions with an efficiency that their opponents never suspected.

Ticonderoga's guns

On the night of May 10, 1775, the small garrison of Fort Ticonderoga was fast asleep when the sentry was startled by knocking at its gate; a messenger had just arrived with an important note for Captain William Delaplace who, once awake, had the gate opened. In an instant, some 160 armed American patriots rushed in and overcame the two officers and 48 soldiers of the British 26th Regiment of Foot. Originally built by the French from 1755, the fort (which had been partly destroyed, and then repaired by the British) contained a large quantity of ordnance, including heavy guns. Several days later, the nine soldiers detached at Crown Point on the southern end of Lake Champlain also surrendered. The capture by the patriots of these weakly garrisoned forts, especially Ticonderoga, was to have major strategic consequences.

In June, George Washington, a Virginia officer who had distinguished himself during the campaigns of the Seven Years War, was appointed by Congress to the role of commander-in-chief of the Continental Army, which he joined at Boston in early July. Many of the men in his army now wished to return home to attend to their farms and businesses upon the expiry of their short-term enlistments, but enough remained to maintain an effective blockade around Boston. After Bunker Hill, the British were not keen to attack American lines and redoubts; months of sporadic skirmishing passed while Washington sought to break the deadlock. His army had little artillery and ammunition, but the recent capture of Fort Ticonderoga, replete with ordnance, could change that. Henry Knox was sent to the fort and, from December 1775 to early March 1776, about 60 heavy cannons and mortars with ammunition were hauled and dragged across rivers and snow-covered mountains for some 300 miles until they finally reached the American lines outside Boston.

General Washington and his officers wanted to end the siege's deadlock by occupying Dorchester Heights and building batteries of heavy artillery there; this position commanded the harbor and city of Boston even more effectively than the Charlestown Peninsula. On the night of March 4, some 1,200 American troops suddenly moved in and started work on substantial fortifications in the darkness, their noise being covered by an all-night cannonade initiated by the Americans to fool the British. Since the ground was still frozen, it could not be dug. Occasional engineer Rufus Putman came up with a solution seen in a borrowed copy of *Muller's Field Engineer*: making "chandeliers" whose timber frames were laid over the ground and

The "Noble Train of Artillery," December 1775 – a painting by Tom Lovell. The American surprise capture of Fort Ticonderoga on May 10, 1775, included its numerous pieces of heavy artillery. From December 1775 to the end of January 1776, American artillery commander Henry Knox managed to have some 60 tons of ordnance hauled in an epic journey to General George Washington's army blockading the British troops in Boston. By early March, American batteries around Boston had the heavy guns. As a result, the British evacuated the city on March 17. (Joseph Dixon Crucible Company, Jersey City, NJ/Fort Ticonderoga Museum, Ticonderoga, NY; author's photograph)

filled with earth and other material such as "a vast number of large bundles of screwed hay" brought by some 360 oxcarts. These works were strengthened, notably with "a great number of barrels, filled with stones and sand, arranged in front of our works; which are to be put in motion and made to roll down the hill, to break the ranks and legs of the assailants as they advance," recalled James Tatcher. By early morning, the dismayed British in Boston could clearly see artillery positions on Dorchester Heights that had been, when last seen the evening before, grass-covered pasture.

Bombardment would soon make Boston untenable and General Gage ordered Lord Percy to attack Dorchester Heights with 3,000 men at once. However, nature also intervened in the form of a heavy storm that made crossing the army by boat impossible. By March 5, it was clear that the Americans had made the earth and timber fortifications almost impregnable. Howe cancelled the order to attack and concluded that the only way to

New York City and the Hudson River

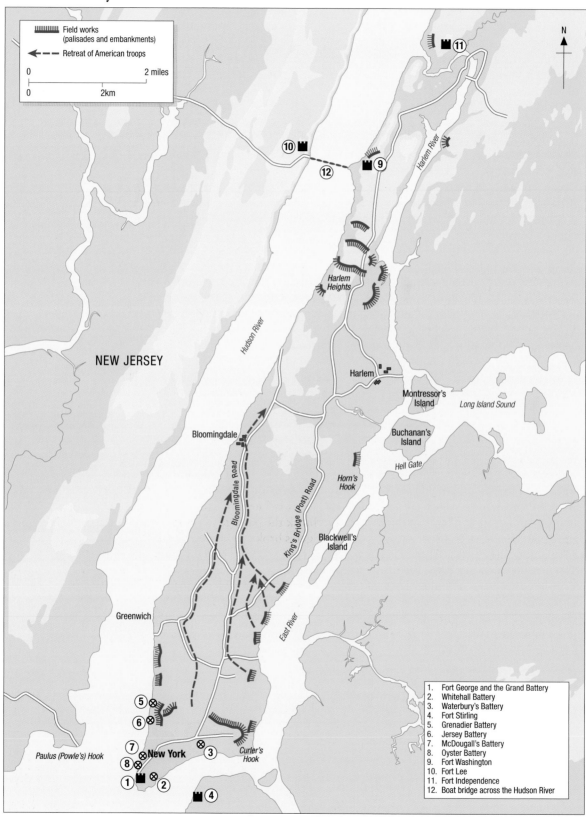

Field works
(palisades and embankments)

Retreat of American troops

0   2 miles

0   2km

N

NEW JERSEY

Hudson River

Harlem
Heights

Harlem

Montressor's
Island

Long Island Sound

Buchanan's
Island

Bloomingdale

Hell Gate

Horn's
Hook

Blackwell's
Island

King's Bridge (Post) Road

Bloomingdale Road

Greenwich

East River

Paulus (Powle's) Hook

New York

Curler's
Hook

1. Fort George and the Grand Battery
2. Whitehall Battery
3. Waterbury's Battery
4. Fort Stirling
5. Grenadier Battery
6. Jersey Battery
7. McDougall's Battery
8. Oyster Battery
9. Fort Washington
10. Fort Lee
11. Fort Independence
12. Boat bridge across the Hudson River

save his army was to evacuate Boston. He advised the Americans not to intervene or he would destroy the city; Washington's gamble with Ticonderoga's guns, which had not even fired a round, and making Dorchester Heights' earth and timber fortifications formidable paid off handsomely and an armistice was agreed. On March 17, some 12,000 soldiers, Loyalists and their dependents sailed out of Boston after dismantling old Castle William, which guarded the harbor's access.

The fortifications of New York and Manhattan, 1776–83

The British fleet that evacuated Boston in late March 1776 went to Halifax. By that time, the British government had made arrangements to send more troops and ships to North America while it reaffirmed its policy of subduing the rebellion. New regiments were raised, Loyalists were armed, and German mercenary troops hired. In July, a large British fleet with about 32,000 troops led by General Sir William Howe on board anchored in lower New York Bay. The British objective was to occupy New York City and control the Hudson River Valley. Howe's troops were landed on Long Island and, on August 26, defeated the weaker Continental Army under General Washington, who averted annihilation by withdrawing north to forts Lee and Washington in the Harlem Heights area. In mid-September, the Americans evacuated New York City – its old Fort George, with a few shore and island batteries, being easily vulnerable to a force such as General Howe's. Because of its excellent strategic position, New York City became the headquarters of the British forces in North America; henceforth, a substantial number of army troops and Royal Navy ships would always be stationed on Manhattan Island and in its immediate area. Furthermore, many field fortifications were built by the British and German troops, especially just around the Harlem Heights area.

The Americans dug in too. They were determined not to allow the British to gain control of the Hudson River Valley. Fort Washington, to the north of Harlem Heights, was a large, bastioned earth and wood structure built on a rectangular plan on an eminence overlooking the Hudson River. Just across the Hudson River on the New Jersey shore was Fort Lee; both forts were connected by a boat bridge that also served to block the passage of shipping north on the river. On October 9, two British frigates broke through the boat bridge, proving the Americans could not bar the passage. Three days later,

A British hut camp on the outskirts of New York City, c.1776–83, in a print after J. W. Dunsmore in R. P. Bolton's *Relics of the Revolution … on Manhattan Island* (1916). The camp shown here was at Dunmore Farm in northern Manhattan. (Author's collection)

General Howe bypassed the northern end of Manhattan, eventually chasing Washington's troops as far as White Plains (also known as Chatterton's Hill) where he lost about 230 British soldiers before taking American entrenchments. Howe then turned south, detached part of his troops on the New Jersey shore, and moved on to forts Washington and Lee. Fort Washington was the main American work and about 3,000 men were posted there. It remained, however, unfinished,

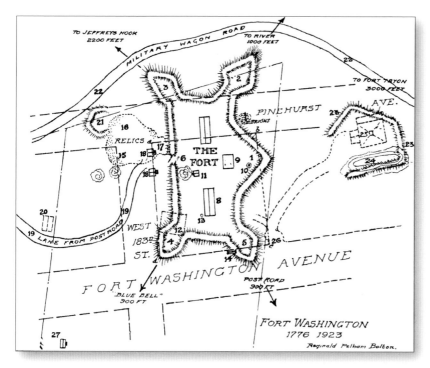

An outline of Fort Washington, 1776–83, from W. L. Carver and R. P. Bolton's *History Written with Pick and Shovel* (1950). Built by the Americans at the northern end of Manhattan Island, it was captured by British and Hessian troops and renamed Fort Knyphausen. This map was based on archaeological surveys made in the early 20th century. (Author's collection)

having no outer defenses (other than isolated redoubts), deep ditches, or ravelins; it was thus actually a weak citadel armed with 34 cannons and two howitzers. Several redoubts were located in the area around the fort, notably to the south, the most vulnerable side for an infantry assault. Sensing it could not resist, General Washington had asked for the fort to be evacuated, but General Nathanael Greene delayed and, by November 15, it was too late. Howe's superior army assisted by Royal Navy warships invested the place and, the following day, British and German troops mounted a general assault under the command of General Wilhelm von Knyphausen. At length, the latter succeeded in overcoming the stubborn resistance of the garrison. Once again, Americans protected by field works inflicted some 500 casualties on the attackers, compared to their own losses of about 150; however, over 3,000 Americans were made prisoner. Regrettably, some enraged German soldiers slaughtered a few prisoners before they could be stopped; it is said that General Washington was watching from the opposite shore and wept when he saw the slaughter. As a result of the fall of Fort Washington, Fort Lee across the river was evacuated. The Americans thus suffered a major setback and the British now controlled the lower Hudson River Valley.

The American forces retreated further north and built forts Clinton and Montgomery on high ground bordering the west bank of the Hudson about 40 miles from New York City. They also laid a chain across the river. Of these

A View of the Attack against Fort Washington and Rebel Redoubts near New York on the 16 of November 1776 by the British and Hessian Brigades, a watercolor after Thomas Davies. Fort Washington is the long narrow rectangle on top of the hill at the center of the picture. The outlying redoubts are also shown with smoke arising from them. (Courtesy Yale University Art Gallery, New London, CT)

The "eagle's nest" location of Fort Putnam, one of the southern defenses of West Point, is clearly shown in this detail of an 1825 painting by Thomas Cole of the fort's substantial ruins. (Philadelphia Museum of Fine Art; author's photograph)

earthen forts reinforced with timber and stone, Fort Montgomery, built on a triangular plan, was both the most extensive and impressive, being situated on a 1,000ft-high cliff. The forts were still under construction when, on October 3, 1777, Sir Henry Clinton leading 3,000 British and German troops headed north. He secured Stoney Point early on October 6 and proceeded to attack and take both American forts from the landward side. The forts were then destroyed. Sir Henry's troops went as far as Kingston along the Hudson, ravaging towns along the way, but then turned back seeing that many more American troops were mobilizing to surround his force. Thus vanished the last British hope of putting pressure on the southern flank of General Gates' American army that was closing in on General John Burgoyne's British and German army trapped at Saratoga (see later).

The Americans regrouped and, in January 1778, established their Hudson Highlands stronghold at West Point, a natural fortress with an imposing cliff overlooking the western shore of the Hudson River 55 miles north of New York City. Here they built a new fort (initially called Arnold and later changed to Clinton) whose landward southern and western earthen curtain walls were 9ft high and 20ft thick with bases revetted with stone. There were also three redoubts and batteries to the south named forts Meigs, Wyllys, and Webb along with Fort Putman and Rocky Hill, a strong outer redoubt. The Shelburne redoubt was west of Fort Clinton. Across the river were three batteries to the north and, further inland to the southeast, the North and the South redoubts. A floating boat bridge linked both shores. An important feature was a chain laid across the river, and further obstacles were placed in the water to prevent uncontrolled navigation. West Point was also home to the Continental Army's engineering school, as well as warehouses, making it a major supply center for the American army. These works were designed by Louis de la Radière and completed by Tadeusz Kosciuszko, both of whom had studied engineering in France before being commissioned in the Continental Army.

In late May 1779, Sir Henry Clinton again exited New York City with about 6,000 men hoping to secure the Hudson Highlands. In early June, his force occupied Stoney Point, whose 40-man American garrison set fire

to their blockhouse before fleeing north. The British built an earth fortification with outer abatis on a rocky height only vulnerable from the west and armed it with 15 pieces of ordnance. Failing to goad General Washington into a general engagement, the British returned to New York leaving about 650 men to garrison Stoney Point. Washington then ordered General Anthony Wayne to capture it. On July 15, he marched down from West Point towards his objective with 1,300 men. The work built on a rocky height was protected by the Hudson River to the east, north, and south, and by swamps to the west. It was taken by a well-executed, surprise bayonet assault after midnight on July 16. Lieutenant-Colonel François Fleury, an occasional engineer and also battalion commander, was the first man to enter the enemy works, sword in hand, and he boldly pulled down the British flag. Its capture provided great encouragement to American morale and was widely reported upon, although it was abandoned two days later because Washington did not have enough troops. It was reoccupied and strengthened by the British, but its importance was diminished.

The British, too, were short of men in New York. An American raid took place before dawn on August 19 on the British redoubts at Paulus (Powle's) Hook (now Jersey City) just across from New York City. Major Henry Lee made a surprise bayonet attack over the abatis and ditch, took its two redoubts – each of which had a blockhouse – without a shot, and immediately withdrew with 158 prisoners. In the fall of 1779, the positions they had taken from the Americans at the northern end of Manhattan and the heights bordering the eastern shore of the East River were evacuated by the British, who demolished all fortifications above a new defensive "line of circumvallation" built across the island. Thereafter, the tactical situation in the New York area remained at a standstill since the main focus of the war had moved from the northern to the middle and southern states.

Although the British could not take formidable West Point by the sword, they tried to do so by treachery. In July 1780, the leading American general Benedict Arnold, embittered by a perceived lack of recognition, proposed to betray his command, West Point, and his substantial garrison to the British. However, on September 23, the plot was discovered when a civilian, revealed to be British Major John

"View of the British Fortress at Stoney-Point [New York], stormed and carried by a party of the Light Corps of the American Army, under the command of Gen. WAYNE, on the Morning of 16th of July last [1779]." This crude print, published in 1779, is one of the rare American renderings showing an assault on a fortified position. The marker A denotes "The British fortress." The reserve is shown at bottom left, while the "detached Party who stormed the Works" can be seen above them. (Courtesy Library of Congress, Washington)

American General Benedict Arnold boards the Royal Navy sloop HMS *Vulture* on September 24, 1780, fleeing from the consequences of his failed attempt to deliver the United States' fortress at West Point to the British forces. When the plot was discovered, Arnold escaped to the Hudson River, and took refuge on the British ship. He later served as a general against his compatriots, earning for himself universal and ongoing scorn as a traitor to all Americans. A print after Howard Pyle. (Author's collection)

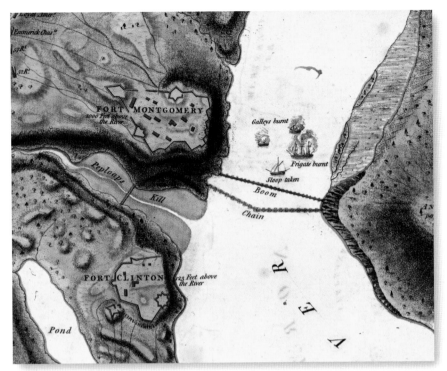

Plans of forts Montgomery and Clinton, 1777 – a detail from a map by John Hill. These American forts were taken by the British on October 6. Both consisted of earth and timber walls built on irregular plans, and featured an inside redoubt. Fort Montgomery was built on a cliff 1,000ft above the Hudson River; Fort Clinton was much lower at 123ft elevation. (Courtesy Library of Congress, Washington)

André, was stopped by American militiamen and found to be in possession of compromising documents. Arnold managed to escape, André was hung as a spy, and the "American Gibraltar" was saved.

The result was that some 10,000 British regular troops remained isolated in the area of New York City and its immediate outer areas. Protecting the most strategically important British military base in North America remained crucial. A strong garrison was necessary since New York was permanently surrounded by at least a dozen Continental Army regiments assisted by cavalry, artillery, and, at times, militia regiments. There was also an internal security worry since it was suspected that a substantial part of the population was sympathetic to the American case.

The Mohawk Valley and Saratoga

In 1777, General Sir John Burgoyne was to carry out a grand plan to crush the rebellion in New York and adjacent states accompanied by the utter defeat and ruin of the Continental Army. He would personally lead an 8,000-man army south from Canada; a secondary force of 2,000 men would approach from the west and secure the Mohawk River Valley; General Sir William Howe would come up the Hudson from New York. The meeting point was Albany. The details of the utter failure of the plan and its disastrous consequences for the British cause regarding American independence, which had been proclaimed since July 4, 1776, are well known. Here we shall focus on the role of fortification in what amounted to three separate campaigns.

Howe, seemingly through a lack of effective communication, headed south from New York City with 15,000 troops in late July 1777 to attack Philadelphia instead of going north. When, in early October, General Sir Henry Clinton moved north from New York City, it was too little and too late.

At Oswego, Lieutenant-Colonel Barry St Leger commanded a force of some 1,700 mostly Loyalist troops that included several hundred Mohawk warriors led by Chief Joseph Brant, all of which reached Fort Stanwix (that had been renamed Fort Schuyler, now Rome, NY) on the north shore of the Mohawk River on August 3. This was a large earth and timber fort built since 1758 on a square plan with bastions. It had a garrison of 750 American troops under the command of Colonel Peter Gansevoort. The British simply had to take this imposing work in order to proceed east towards Albany. As it was, communities along the Mohawk River were solidly loyal to the American cause and had already often suffered from raiding parties of British Loyalists and Mohawk Indians, the latter largely at the behest of Sir John Johnson, whose still-standing mansion guarded by two masonry blockhouses at Johnstown had previously been seized by the "rebels." Fort Stanwix was blockaded since St Leger did not have siege artillery to pound it into submission. Meanwhile, elderly militia General Nicholas Herkimer sounded the alarm and soon rallied some 800 Tryon County militiamen, who marched to the relief of the fort. On August 6, both sides clashed during a thunderstorm at Oriskany, about 8 miles from the fort, which proved to be one of the hardest-fought hand-to-hand battles of the war. At dusk the patriot militiamen eventually retreated having lost a quarter of their men; the winners had suffered 150 casualties and were too weak to pursue. Hearing the musketry fire, Gansevoort led a sortie from the fort, captured St Leger's nearby camp, and brought back into the fort all the supplies he could. At sunset, the new American standard, the Stars and Stripes, which had just been made in the fort from an old jacket and a petticoat, was hoisted

Blockhouse at Fort Plain, NY, c.1776. Built in 1776 to protect the village of Fort Plain on the northern shore of the Mohawk River against Indian and Loyalist attacks. According to J. W. Barber and H. Howe's *Historical Collections…* (1845), its "form was an octagon, having portholes for heavy ordnance and muskets on every side. It contained three stories or apartments. The first story was thirty feet in diameter; the second, forty feet; the third, fifty feet; the last two stories projecting five feet … It was constructed throughout of hew timber about fifteen inches square; and besides the port-holes aforesaid, the second and third stories had perpendicular port-holes." (Author's collection)

Johnson Hall in the 1760s/1770s, in a painting by Edward L. Henry (1903). The residence of first Sir William Johnson, Superintendent of Indian Affairs, then his son Sir John Johnson, was flanked by two masonry blockhouses. (Albany Institute of History and Art, Albany, NY; author's photograph)

in defiance for the first time over a battlefield. Eventually, General Arnold with 1,200 Americans was sent to raise the siege; as a result, on August 22, St Leger headed back to Canada.

The main army under General Burgoyne left Canada in June. It had 8,000 British and German regulars (nearly all of the latter from the state of Brunswick) accompanied by several hundred Loyalists, Canadian embodied militiamen, and Indians. Nothing stood in its way until it reached the vicinity of Fort Ticonderoga. Burgoyne worried he would be delayed by a formal siege of the old Vauban-style stone fort, but its defenses were crumbling. Nevertheless, the partly sick and poorly supplied 3,000-strong American garrison had built fortifications on Mount Independence overlooking the fort, but not on Sugar Hill, esteemed to be outside artillery range. When Burgoyne's army reached Ticonderoga on June 30, its engineers correctly concluded that it was within range of heavy artillery and, during the next days, batteries of 24pdr cannons and 8in. howitzers were emplaced on top of Sugar Hill. The American troops withdrew on July 6.

A model of Fort Stanwix at the time of its siege in July and August 1777. All the textbook refinements of a substantial earth and wood fort are shown. Only heavy cannons and large mortars could subdue such a work if well defended, but trains of siege artillery were rarely seen in the wilderness. (Fort Stanwix National Monument, Rome, NY; author's photograph)

Until then, Burgoyne's army had travelled by boat, but now had to go through wilderness paths, when there were any, to reach still distant Albany. American opposition was now increasingly present with many skirmishes occurring as the army marched, reaching abandoned Fort Edward on July 30. Thousands of American militiamen and troops in this increasingly populated area were mobilizing to oppose Burgoyne's army. A first major engagement cast a very dark shadow on its fate. Burgoyne sent a 600-man detachment of German troops led by Colonel Baum to seize stores at the village of Bennington, 30 miles southeast of Fort Edward, but, 6 miles from there, the column was surrounded by thousands of Americans under General John Stark on August 16. The Brunswickers dug trenches around their camp and sent out requests for reinforcements. The Americans, many of whom were

Raising the flag of the United States during the siege of Fort Stanwix on August 6, 1777. The American Congress adopted the "Stars and Stripes" national flag in June 1777. It was reportedly made from an old blue jacket and a soldier's wife's petticoat, and first raised at Fort Stanwix following Colonel Willett's victorious sortie against British, Loyalist, and Mohawk Indian besiegers. The scene has been recreated in this 1927 painting. The fort is recreated according to the information then available, but the wilderness shown gives an excellent idea of where North American forts were located. (Fort Stanwix National Monument, Rome, NY; author's photograph)

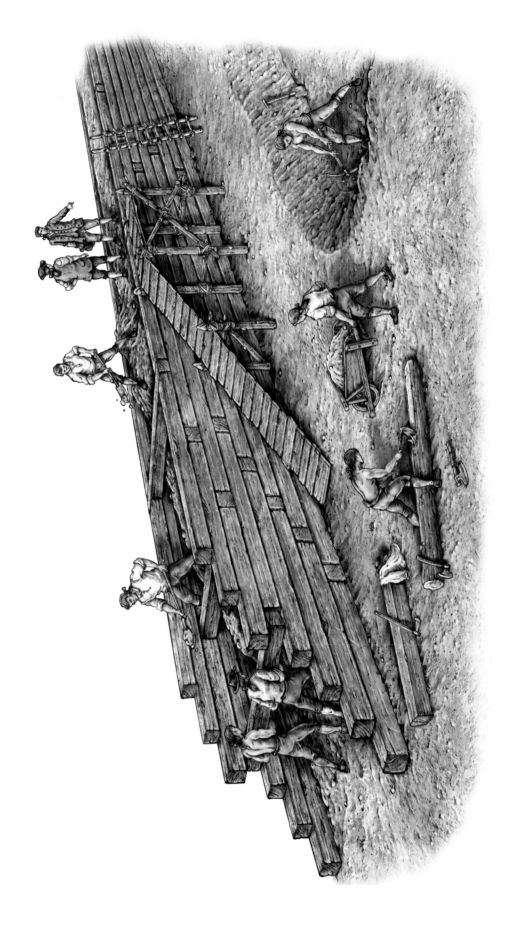

Fort Ticonderoga in 1777, a detail from a contemporary map. The fort was reoccupied by General John Burgoyne's British Army on July 6, 1777, its American garrison having evacuated the site the previous day. Burgoyne's army added "New Lines" on the west side next to the older works built by the French during the 1750s. It then moved on, leaving a garrison which was blockaded by American troops. Following Burgoyne's surrender at Saratoga on October 17, the garrison of Ticonderoga largely destroyed the fort and its works before retreating to Canada in November. (Courtesy, Library of Congress, Washington)

excellent shots with rifles and hunting muskets, poured a tremendous fire from covered positions, to which the German soldiers replied; the Americans' accurate shooting decided the issue and the Germans surrendered after two hours. Sometime later, a relief force of about 550 Brunswick troops led by Colonel Heinrich von Breymann appeared; Stark's men fell back, but General Seth Warner's numerous American reinforcements now arrived on the scene. Breymann's troops fled and isolated riflemen shot at them all the way back to Fort Edward. This showed that European professional soldiers, even protected by field fortifications in a wilderness setting, could be vanquished by accurate small-arms fire. Burgoyne now went to Duer, a secured position between Fort Edward and Saratoga, to regroup his army and gather supplies. Meanwhile, American troops kept arriving in the area, somewhat loosely under the command of elderly General Horatio Gates, whose army eventually numbered as many as 16,000 men. One of his staff officers was engineer Tadeusz Kosciuszko. He had already delayed the advance of Burgoyne's army

B **CONSTRUCTION OF AN EARTH AND TIMBER FORTIFICATION**

Fortifications made of timber and earth were very common and almost the only type constructed in North America during the War of Independence. They certainly would not last a long time, but could be erected in a relatively short time if there were enough men to do the work.

The most basic type was the horizontal timber wall, which called for squared logs laid one above the other in two parallel rows with timbers making a "basket work" connecting them for solidity. The empty space between was filled with earth (or other earthy material such as sand and small rocks depending on what was locally available) resulting in a substantial curtain wall that was effective against enemy artillery fire. The construction details could vary greatly depending on circumstances, sites, materials available, and time allowed to build. For instance, the squared logs could be laid on one side,

earth stacked up and ending in an abrupt slope whose perpendicular angle would then be revetted on the outside by stacking rectangles of sod (measuring about 3in. x 12in. x 18in.) held in place by small wooden pickets driven through and with the grassy side laid under and not above. Such walls would also have banquettes and artillery platforms with ordnance firing through embrasures made of the same materials.

There could be many other variations. For instance, in warmer climates, bricks could also be used instead of timber. This type of fortification may seem crude compared to fine masonry fortresses, but it provided good protection even under intense cannon fire. With outside ditches and glacis, such forts, be they closed field redoubts or bastioned works, were effective strongholds that required considerable effort to overcome and could render horrendous casualties to assault troops in the process.

A plan view of the American fortifications on Bemis Heights, late September 1777. General Gates' headquarters is at lower left; the Bemis Tavern is at the upper right near the Hudson River (shown in light blue). This reconstruction was mainly made from archaeological finds and surviving terrain features. (Saratoga National Historic Site, National Park Service, Saratoga, NY; author's photograph)

by felling trees across the roads and by having all bridges destroyed. Now he identified the area of Bemis Heights, south of Saratoga, on the west bank of the upper Hudson River, as a site on which to build large-scale field fortifications that could stop Burgoyne's advance on Albany. These fortifications combined extensive earthen and wood lines laid out in a zigzag pattern with outer abatis and numerous outer redoubts. Their eastern side ended on a bluff that commanded the road to Albany and the Hudson River.

Meanwhile, General Burgoyne's army crossed to the west bank of the Hudson River on September 13 and a few days later arrived in the area of the American position some 4 miles to the north. The land between the two armies was a mixture of woodland and cleared fields, one of which was called Freeman's Farm. On September 19, Burgoyne's columns advanced, seemingly expecting to carry the American positions fairly easily. However, the Americans put up great resistance in the fields and nearly outflanked the British troops, who finally managed to repulse them. They built field fortifications for protection against possible American raids. In the following weeks, General Burgoyne remained somewhat uncertain as to which course to follow, while General Gates was even more cautious. Then, on October 7, a British reconnaissance force in the woods was met by American troops; the skirmish developed into a full-scale action on the western flank of the British works. The Americans failed to take the Balcarres Redoubt, which had a peculiar elongated shape, but they also attacked the most westerly position held by Colonel Breymann and his Brunswick grenadiers. The Breymann "redoubt" was actually simply a line of logs laid vertically on a height to the north of Freeman's Farm. General Arnold leading the Americans managed to outflank the defenders and storm the position; during the fighting Colonel Breymann was killed. Its fall was critical in that Americans would now be closing in around Burgoyne's army. The talented and popular British General

A model of the field of Saratoga in October 1777. This view is seen from the north. The British camp, defense lines, batteries, and redoubts are in the foreground, with those of the Americans further away. (Saratoga National Historic Site, National Park Service, Saratoga, NY; author's photograph)

Simon Fraser was also mortally wounded by an American rifleman that day. Thereafter, things looked increasingly grim for the British Army, but Burgoyne did not move; his army was surrounded as of October 13. The British Army could hold out in the relative safety of its field fortifications, but it was now completely cut off and, with no hope of relief, Burgoyne surrendered on October 17. It was one of the greatest victories in American history: a whole army made up of professional British and German troops, which had never been able to even approach, let alone attack, the American field fortifications on Bemis Heights, now laid down arms. Not only did Saratoga greatly encourage the Americans, but it convinced France to enter the war on the side of the United States.

Breymann's Redoubt attacked by American troops at Saratoga, October 7, 1777. Having first failed to take the Balcarres Redoubt, the Americans attacked the defensive position now known as Breymann's Redoubt, named after the commander of the Brunswick grenadiers that defended what was really no more than a crude barrier of logs laid horizontally. The determined American frontal assaults were supported by a successful flank attack led by General Arnold, who was wounded and lost a leg in the action. This diorama is at Saratoga National Historic Site, National Park Service, Saratoga, NY. (Author's photograph)

Philadelphia

Meanwhile, General Washington's and General Howe's armies fought several battles, chiefly in Pennsylvania, but without being able to destroy each other's force. These were largely field engagements involving minimal use of fortifications. One of the British objectives was the largely unfortified city of Philadelphia, then the capital of the United States. On September 26, 1777, General Charles Cornwallis, second-in-command to Howe, entered the city with part of the British Army to the acclamation, it should be added, of several thousand Loyalist inhabitants. However, the Continental Army was not destroyed and was lurking outside the city, so a line of defensive earthworks with ten redoubts stretching from the Schuylkill River to the Delaware River was built by the British north of the city. The Americans also held forts Mifflin and Mercer that commanded naval access to Philadelphia by the Delaware River south of the city. Fort Mifflin, situated on Mud Island, had been built in 1771 under the direction of British engineer John Montresor. It was an especially strong work with an innovative design having its southeast curtain wall echeloned in succeeding bastions to provide increased firepower on river traffic that could also crossfire with the smaller pentagonal Fort Mercer on the opposite, eastern shore. These American-held forts, with their supporting smaller works, simply had to be taken by the British to secure their naval communications to Philadelphia. On November 22, a force of 1,200 German troops from Hesse-Cassel under Colonel Carl von Donop moved toward Fort Mercer with its garrison of 400 Rhode Island troops under Colonel Christopher Greene. It had just been reinforced with earthworks 10ft high faced with planks with a deep ditch and abatis designed by Thomas-Antoine, chevalier de Mauduit du Plessis, a young French officer who had joined the American cause. Greene felt there was no point sacrificing his garrison at

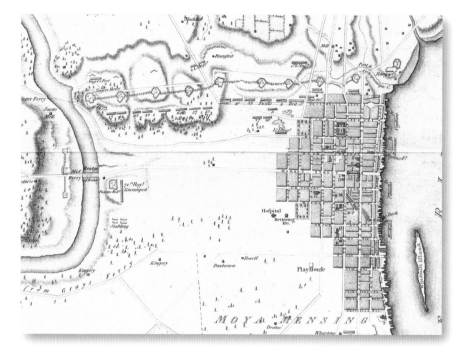

Philadelphia in 1778, taken from a map published in London on January 1, 1779. Philadelphia had no fortifications, so the British Army built a line of field fortifications featuring ten redoubts north of the city between the Schuylkill and Delaware rivers, where most of the troops were encamped. (Courtesy Richard H. Brown Revolutionary War Map Collection, Boston Public Library)

the outworks, and so had them dismantled, deciding to make a stand at Fort Mercer instead. The Hessians' assault was heroic due to the enormous difficulties they encountered trying to cross du Plessis' fortifications, but was doomed when American armed galleys in the river poured enfilading artillery fire on their columns. Von Donop was mortally wounded and about 400 of his men were killed, wounded, or missing, while the Americans suffered about 40 casualties.

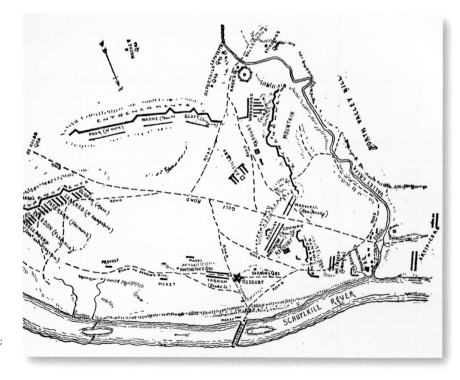

The camp of the Continental Army at Valley Forge, 1777–78. The southern side of the camp was protected by outer entrenchment lines manned by troops from the various states as indicated. More entrenchments and redoubts were in the vicinity of Washington's headquarters (at lower right). (Private collection; author's photograph)

The British command then decided to take Fort Mifflin, the key to all the American positions on the river. They moved into nearby Carpenter's and Providence islands and set up batteries to the west of the fort. Joined by six Royal Navy warships, an intense bombardment rained projectiles on Fort Mifflin from November 10 to 15. By the evening of the 15th, its 400-strong garrison had suffered some 250 casualties and the fort's works "were entirely beat down; every piece of cannon entirely dismounted," as General Washington later wrote; he added that its "defense will always reflect the highest honor upon the officers and men of the garrison," which were led by Major Samuel Thayer. The American flag remained flying over the fort while the garrison evacuated that night. General Howe then sent Cornwallis, at the head of some 5,500 troops, to secure the eastern shore of the Delaware River, including Fort Mercer, which was also evacuated. The British now had naval access to the former American capital, whose modest fortifications had nevertheless provided numerous obstacles for the attackers. Once again, the Americans had shown they could be a formidable opponent in defensive positions.

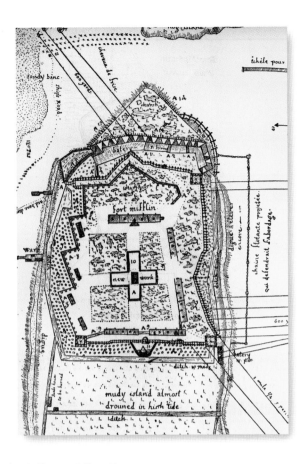

Fort Mifflin, November 9, 1777, in a drawing made by Major Louis Fleury, a French officer with the American garrison, a day before the start of the British bombardment. The south is at top. The plan shows the fort's substantial gun positions on its walls and at the outer battery facing the Delaware River, since it was originally designed to protect Philadelphia from a hostile naval force. Its weaker side, as shown by the many lines (at right) coming from the west, was exposed to British shore batteries. Fleury was later present at Yorktown as a major in the Saintonge French infantry regiment. (Private collection; author's photograph)

Washington's Continental Army was, at that point, the only viable field force that could oppose the British and German troops, and it retired to the hills at Valley Forge, northwest of Philadelphia, for the winter of 1777/78. Like a Roman general, Washington always fortified any place that his army occupied and, being a former surveyor in his younger years, helped lay out various field works that made Valley Forge next to impregnable. The victory at Saratoga had been great news, but food, medication, uniforms, and warm clothes were in short supply for the soldiers huddled in crude wooden huts in the snow that winter at Valley Forge. By early February 1778, nearly 4,000 men were sick while others, famished, had deserted or were so discouraged they were near to mutiny. However, through it all the will to fight rarely wavered; the remarkable work of another professional officer, Baron Friedrich von Steuben, former staff officer to King Frederick the Great of Prussia, relentlessly drilling and training the Continental soldiers during the winter brought the Americans to a hitherto unseen level of discipline, efficiency, and capacity to maneuver on the field on par with contemporary European armies whilst preserving the effective American light-infantry fighting methods.

Furthermore, France's recognition of the United States in February 1778 brought much encouragement to the colonies, for it promised substantial material, monetary, and manpower assistance would eventually be forthcoming. However, recalling the events of the Seven Years War, many Americans must have fervently hoped that the French Navy and Army would perform better when hostilities began between France and Britain, which they did in July 1778. By then, Valley Forge, which had never been approached by British troops, had been abandoned. Contrary to expectations, the entry

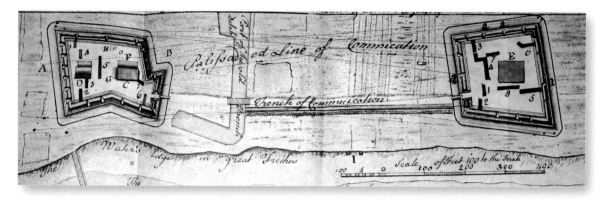

A plan of Fort St John (or Saint-Jean), 1775. In September, both redoubts were completed and armed with about 30 pieces of artillery, amongst which were two 8in. howitzers, eight Royal or Coehorn mortars, two 24pdr brass cannons and six 9pdr iron cannons; other weapons were of small caliber. (Courtesy Library and Archives Canada)

of France into the conflict necessitated the evacuation of Philadelphia, the British Army leaving the city on June 18, 1778, to regroup at New York: the British command needed to reinforce and concentrate its forces in case a squadron from the new and powerful French fleet intervened in America. Indeed, the French went on the offensive in the West Indies, gaining several victories against the British, who were forced to send reinforcements from New York to the islands; to compound matters, sudden fear of a French invasion gripped Great Britain itself. Seeing General Clinton abandon Philadelphia, General Washington attacked the British rearguard at Monmouth, New Jersey. Clinton ordered a counterattack and American General Charles Lee, lacking confidence that his troops could stand against British regulars, ordered a retreat of some 15 miles. Lee's withdrawal ended when a furious Washington ordered Lee off the battlefield, and formed a line that, assisted by a battery on a hill, stopped and then forced the British to withdraw to New York City the same night. The fighting at Monmouth showed that the Continental Army trained by von Steuben could hold its own in an open field as well as behind earthworks.

CANADA

In September 1775, while the siege of Boston was in progress, General Washington detached 1,000 infantrymen with three companies of riflemen under General Benedict Arnold from his army to advance to Quebec through the forests of Maine. There, they would join General Richard Montgomery's army of about 2,000 men that was invading Canada by Lake Champlain and the Richelieu River; the plan was for Montgomery's troops to take Montreal and then march on Quebec. As it turned out, the daring plan to conquer Canada ran into difficulties caused by fortifications. Montgomery's army had no opposition until September 6 when it came to Saint-Jean, or St John, on the west bank of the Richelieu River. Since 1665, this place had been the site of several successive French forts that were in ruins by 1775.

Saint-Jean
Anticipating a possible American foray, Sir Guy Carleton, governor of Canada, had tasked Major Charles Preston of the 26th Foot to have fortifications built at Saint-Jean. Preston, who knew this had to be done quickly, chose to erect two strong redoubts connected by a 700ft-long "trench of communication." These works were built by 300 men from July to

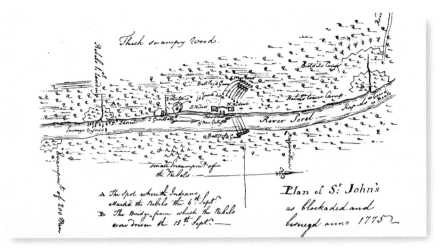

The siege of Fort St John, September 1775. Three American batteries bombard the two redoubts that form the fort. (Courtesy Library and Archives Canada)

September and armed with some 30 guns. While the Americans landed south of the fort, a party of First Nations warriors (indigenous Canadians not part of the Inuit and Métis) allied to the British ambushed them, killing several before withdrawing. The Americans persisted during the following days and invested the fort. The siege started on September 18; some 567 men, mostly from the 7th and the 26th regiments with some Canadian militiamen, garrisoned the redoubts. There were also about 700 women and children seeking refuge, so that some 1,300 people were huddled in those two small redoubts. These were strong enough to discourage the Continental Army from attempting an assault and the Americans strived instead to secure the immediate area, notably by occupying nearby Fort Chambly on October 18, where they found ample ammunition and supplies. Initially, the artillery in the redoubts was far superior to the few guns the Americans had and the British and Canadians could fire ten shots to every American round.

Although Major Preston and his troops were relatively secure in these earth and wood redoubts, they were totally isolated with little hope of relief since there were few regular soldiers left in Montreal or Quebec. The Americans realized that the only way to take Saint-Jean without risking high casualties in an assault was to pound it with relentless artillery bombardments. This would take precious time, but it was the only sensible course of action. Consequently, some of the heavy guns at Fort Ticonderoga were brought up to Saint-Jean and three batteries were built, for a total of eight mortars and ten cannons. The effect to those in the redoubts was soon apparent. Canadian militiaman Foucher mentioned that, on November 1, the Americans fired about a thousand rounds on the fort, many of them mortar bombs. The weather was rainy and the damaged earthen redoubts were very muddy. By then, there was hardly any ammunition left and rations to feed the 1,300 besieged would only last a few days more. Major Preston now felt he had resisted all he could. On November 3, Fort Saint-Jean surrendered after a valiant defense. Its resistance was remarkable considering it consisted of only

A model of Fort St John in 1775, at the Musée du Fort Saint-Jean, Saint-Jean (Quebec). The fort consisted of two redoubts linked by a trench or covered way. (Author's collection)

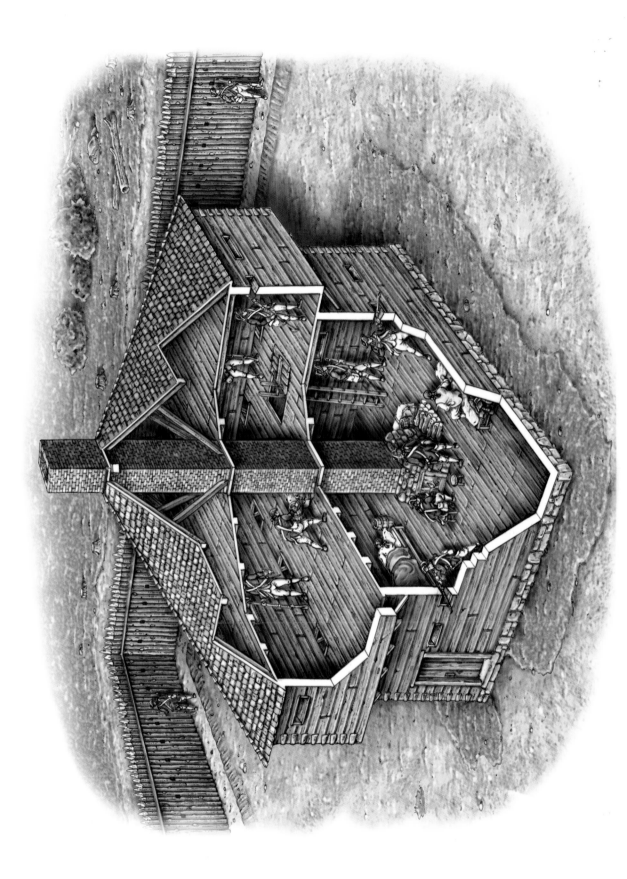

Detail from *A South West View of St John's, August 1779* – a watercolor by James Hunter. The two redoubts are on the west side of the Richelieu River, with the northern redoubt clearly shown and the southern one only faintly. After the British reoccupied the area in 1776, the eastern bank was also secured, as witnessed by the blockhouse in a redoubt in the left foreground. (Courtesy Library and Archives Canada, C1507)

two redoubts, and it delayed Montgomery's plans to conquer Canada in the fall. Now, the weather was becoming colder and the severe rigors of a Canadian winter were rapidly approaching. Ten days later, the Continental Army entered Montreal; the few defending troops left had retreated with Governor Carleton to the fortress of Quebec.

Quebec

Meanwhile, General Arnold and about 700 men arrived in front of the fortress city on November 15 after a grueling trek through the wilderness and, on December 3, Montgomery and his troops joined them. The American army then stood at about 2,000 men and it set up its camp on the Plains of Abraham, on the west side of the fortress. In the city were 1,120 defenders of which some 800 were militiamen, the rest being sailors, artificers, recruits, and a company of regulars of the 7th Royal Fusiliers.

For generals Montgomery and Arnold, the crucial problem facing them was how to attack Quebec city. There was no crumbling and inadequate curtain wall surrounding the city, as there had been at Montreal – Quebec was one of the mightiest fortresses in the Americas thanks chiefly to its location on Cape Diamond. Its constructed fortifications were not especially formidable or extensive and it did not even have a powerful masonry citadel featuring all the latest refinements. The modest walls surrounding the 17th-century Château Saint-Louis, residence of the governor general of Canada, would not make much of a redoubt despite being called a "citadel"

C TIMBER BLOCKHOUSE

Blockhouses, whose north European origins are obscure, were seen as early as 1622 in Plymouth Pilgrim Colony and spread to other English colonies. They were ideal self-contained, small strongholds that could be rapidly put up with logs, or squared timbers if there was more time to build. Both the Americans and the British used them extensively during the American War of Independence. They were usually built on a square or rectangular plan, two stories high, the second story overhanging with a sloped roof, and containing loopholes for muskets, windows that became portholes for ordnance, and machicolation in the overhang to permit defenders to direct a downward fire. Since they were living quarters, they had a chimney with fireplaces, sleeping bunks, and other implements for the soldiers within. A ladder gave access to the upper story although stars were also seen in large blockhouses. As can be seen in some of the illustrations in this book as well as in many other images, the variations were innumerable including some being made of stone to minimize the risk of being set on fire by a foe. Their outer defenses could be just a stockade or much more elaborate earthworks making them the strongest part of a redoubt. Blockhouses could also form the integral part of the walls of a frontier fort acting as turrets or be outside the curtain walls of a large work. The many purposes these buildings served explains their great popularity in North American warfare.

Plan of the siege and blockade of Quebec, from December 8, 1775 to May 13, 1776. From April 1776, the Americans had three modest batteries (visible at left, top and right) to bombard the city. (Courtesy Library of Congress, Washington)

(the scenic Château Frontenac Hotel now occupies the site). Moreover, the initial attempts to build a larger timber and earth citadel on Cape Diamond at the southwestern end of the walls had barely begun in 1775. On the other hand, the masonry curtain walls built by the French were maintained by the British and improved to some extent, notably by finishing the ditches outside the western side. There were various small batteries spread all around the city too. However, what really made Quebec such a mighty fortress was its location on the cape. It was a natural fortress that, like the Rock of Gibraltar, merely needed a modest amount of fortifications to make it almost impregnable.

Quebec has a narrow Lower Town built on a narrow strip of land going from the shore of the St Lawrence River to the foot of the cliff that ascends to the citadel. Many merchants had their residences and warehouses in this lower area, whose hub was the Place Royale and its Notre-Dame-des-Victoires or Lower Town church. There were three shore batteries facing south, of which the bastion-shaped redoubt or Batterie Royale was the most important; in 1775, however, the Americans had arrived by land and so it served little defensive purpose. To get from the Lower Town to the Upper Town built on top of the high and steep cliff, one needed to walk up the Côte du Palais or the Sous le Fort streets, both of which had strongly fortified gates. An important detail was that the private housing in Quebec City was generally made of stone and masonry and therefore sturdier than the brick and wood residences found in most other North American cities. As noted above, the west side had a masonry and bastioned rampart with a ditch in front and clear fields with no buildings; the St Louis and Saint-Jean (or St John) fortified gates controlled access. Montgomery's and Arnold's men were encamped further west of this wall and it was obvious to the Americans that an assault, even on that somewhat weaker side, was near suicidal.

The American commanders carefully considered what to do against such a strong position and came up with a novel and daring plan. An assault would be made at night, in the darkness. Two feints would be made against the western walls of the Upper Town: one to the south of the St Louis Gate and the other against the St John Gate. Simultaneously, two strong columns comprising most of the American troops would make their way along Cape Diamond near the shores of the St Lawrence, secure the Lower Town, and storm the gate leading into the Upper Town at the Bishop's Palace. The first and strongest column under General Arnold would come from the north by Sault-au-Matelot street. The second column would come from the west, pass under the heights of Cape Diamond, secure the Près de Ville and the King's

Shipyard position, then ascend with Arnold's men into the Upper Town. If successful, this plan could indeed deliver hundreds of American troops into the city and subdue the mighty fortress.

Carleton, however, had planned for the possibility of such an attack via the Lower Town. Various obstacles and two barriers had been erected on Sault-au-Matelot street with another, containing some artillery, at Près de Ville. Several American deserters spoke of a Lower Town attack, so the garrison was on high alert. Indeed, in the early hours of December 31, the Americans formed their column and moved in for the attack. It was a dark night and it snowed, which reduced visibility and muffled sound. At about 4.00am, some of Quebec's sentries thought they saw lights in the sky through the storm. Captain Malcolm Fraser saw them too and, although no one knew what they meant, he took no chances and sounded the alarm. Drums started beating and the city's church bells rang. Hearing this, the Americans fired two rockets over Cape Diamond while opening cannon and musket fire on the city's west side; the two feints there were meant to draw attention. Meanwhile, Montgomery and his party were advancing, with some difficulty due to banks of snow below Cape Diamond, on the then

fairly narrow path between the river and the cliff, reaching after some delay the strong picket fence erected at Près de Ville. No defenders were seen and pioneers sawed an opening through it. The Americans went on until they reached a second picket fence, through which another opening was made. Montgomery and his officers emerged through this in the dark not far from a barely visible house nearby. "Push on brave boys, Quebec is ours!" shouted Montgomery, charging in with his officers and a Canadian guide. Seconds later, tremendous cannon and musket fire swept nearly every American near the house; only Aaron Burr – a future American vice president – was left standing, unhurt but dazed. Around him, Montgomery, many officers and the

The death of General Richard Montgomery at the Près de Ville access to Quebec City's Lower Town on the night of December 31, 1775, in a print after C. W. Jeffrey. Canadian militiamen poured musket and cannon fire onto the Americans huddled in the stone buildings. (Author's collection)

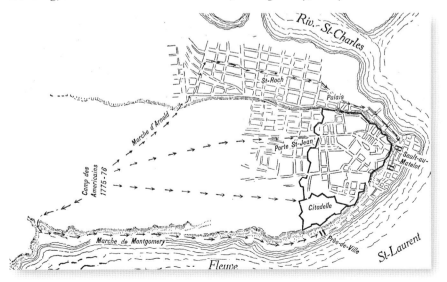

A plan of the American assaults on Quebec City during the night of December 31, 1775, from *Histoire du Canada* (1915). Four columns exit the American camp (*Camp des Américains*) west of the city; two are feints on St John's Gate (*Porte Saint-Jean*) and near the citadel (*Citadelle*) further south, while the other two are the true assault columns led by Arnold to the north and Montgomery to the south. However, both of the latter were to encounter obstacles at Sault-au-Matelot and Près de Ville. (Author's collection)

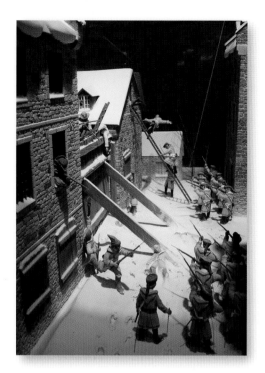

The American attack in Quebec City's Lower Town runs into the second barricade held by Canadian militiamen and British troops on the snowstorm-filled night of December 31, 1775, as depicted in a diorama in the Canadian War Museum, Ottawa. Note the sturdy timber barricade blocking Sault-au-Matelot street between two stone buildings. The defenders repulsed the Americans, who launched further attacks from the rear of their column. (Author's collection)

guide lay dead or dying in the bloodstained snow. The barely visible stone and masonry house had been turned into a redoubt defended by Captain Chabot with about 30 French-Canadian militiamen and a few sailors. The Americans retreated in confusion; the surprise attack had been thwarted by a surprise ambush, and the commanding general had been lost.

This disaster was unknown to General Arnold's main column of about 700 men moving down in the dark from the north towards the center, hampered by snow drifts. When the vanguard of the Americans reached Côte du Palais street, they were spotted by the city's sentries up on the wall, who gave the alarm and fired on them. Arnold, believing that Montgomery was moving in his direction, pressed his men to move on until they reached some cover provided by warehouses. However, a barricade blocked Sault-au-Matelot street, defended by a militia detachment with two small guns that put up a vigorous defense. General Arnold was wounded in the knee before his men withdrew. With Arnold now taken away to the American hospital, Colonel Daniel Morgan led the assault force down the street until he came to a second barricade erected between sturdy stone buildings. While this barricade was stubbornly held by a detachment of the 7th Royal Fusiliers with about 200 Canadian militiamen, Governor Carleton seized the initiative and ordered a counter-attack by a column that charged down from the Côte du Palais, erupting on the flank and rear of Morgan's American troops; they were doomed, and after some sharp fighting in which about 150 were killed or wounded, some 389 surrendered. The British and Canadians suffered at most nine killed and wounded, which gives an idea of how secure they were in the great fortress.

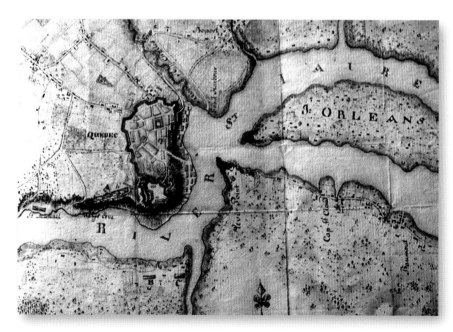

A map of Quebec City and its immediate area, 1780, drawn by Bernard Weiderhold, a German officer in British service. The outline of the wood and earth citadel is clearly visible. (Portuguese Army Library, Lisbon; author's photograph)

Despite the failed assault, the siege by the remaining American force of about 1,000 men, huddled in their camp during the rigors of a Canadian winter, continued. It was a much-weakened force that could, at best, only block access into Quebec. It had few artillery pieces and building batteries was out of the question in winter. For Carleton and his officers, there was no inclination to risk a sortie or attempt skirmishes by raiding parties; the men of the garrison were overwhelmingly city dwellers rather than woodsmen, so it was wiser to hold the fortress until relief came from Britain in the late spring, once the St Lawrence was clear of ice. In the meantime, work continued in the city to strengthen existing defenses. To avoid further surprise attacks from the Americans, the west curtain walls were kept well lit with fires burning from sunset to sunrise; additionally, lanterns tied to poles were extended over the ditches. There was plenty of serviceable ordnance in stores and much of the winter was spent arming the walls. By May 1, 1776, some 148 cannons were mounted and in position. The existing defenses denying access to the Lower Town were also strengthened: at Près de Ville, the nearby iced-in ships moored for the winter were armed with guns thus becoming outer batteries. A wide trench was also cut in the ice from the shore to the open water at the center of the river so that Americans could not outflank the shore defenses by going over the ice. In the Sault-au-Matelot sector, the barricades were strengthened, guns were mounted, and, to secure clear fields of fire, houses lining the street were destroyed.

In the meantime, General Arnold was recovering from his wounds and hardly in a mood to attempt another assault; an unlucky horse fall injured him further and he was relieved by General Wooster on March 31. The Americans kept up the semblance of a siege and, as the milder weather of the early spring appeared in late March and early April, they built three small batteries to harass the city. The battery of four guns and a howitzer at Pointe-Lévis opened up on April 4, with the one on the north shore of the St Charles River comprising only two guns and a howitzer starting on April 22, and a mortar battery on the Plains of Abraham firing its first bombs the following day. However, throughout the siege the artillery mounted on the walls of the city was far superior. According to Sanguinet's account, from December 1775 to May 6, 1776, the Americans fired 784 cannonballs and 180 mainly small mortar bombs into the city wounding only two sailors, with the sole fatality being an unfortunate eight-year-old boy killed by a cannonball. During the same period of time, the city's artillery fired 10,466 cannonballs and 996 mortar bombs towards the Americans. On May 3, the Americans attempted and failed to float a fire ship into the Lower Town harbor. Three days later, the frigate HMS *Surprise* was sighted to the east followed by two more ships; they were the vanguard of a fleet bearing troops

View of the Quebec City walls facing west, a watercolor by James Peachy. The top of St John's Gate (Porte Saint-Jean) and its bastion is seen at center and left. As with the great majority of Quebec's fortifications, the curtain walls, bastions, and gates had been built by French engineers in the 1740s and maintained by the British after 1759. (Courtesy Library and Archives Canada, C1515)

Plan of Fort Cumberland, c.1757. This was the former French Fort Beauséjour until captured by the British in 1755 and renamed Cumberland. Its British garrison was withdrawn in 1768 and it was then reoccupied by Loyalist troops in 1776. It essentially remained the star fort as built by the French, although the British had made a few changes prior to 1768 such as the elimination of the ravelin (P at lower right) and built new barracks outside (H at top). (Fort Beauséjour National Historic Site, Parks Canada; author's photograph)

and supplies from Britain. The British ships moored in Lower Town, and soldiers poured out. Governor Carleton joined them with most of the garrison, which then made a sortie towards the American camp on the Plains. Seeing all this, the Americans panicked and fled, leaving their artillery and even their suppers, which were consumed by British and Canadian troops.

Outside of Quebec City, the overwhelming majority of the population was of French origin and, while small numbers sided with either the Americans or the British, the population remained generally neutral in what appeared to be a fight between their former British and American enemies. Furthermore, American rule in Montreal had not been especially popular; now the British relief force was marching towards Montreal from the east. Meanwhile, British posts on the Great Lakes such as forts Frontenac, Niagara, Detroit, and Mackinac, which had small garrisons, had not been invaded. In May 1776, a mixed party under Captain George Foster of 41 British regulars from the western forts, 210 First Nations allies, and 41 Canadian militiamen was approaching Montreal from the west. On May 18, when this force came to Les Cèdres (or Cedars) on the north shore of the St Lawrence, about 45 miles west of Montreal, it found a small stockade fort recently built there and garrisoned by about 400 American soldiers with two 4lb cannons under the command of Colonel Isaac Butterfield, sent there by General Arnold to guard the western flank of the Continental Army. After some light skirmishing, the Americans – who seem to have especially feared the First Nations warriors – stayed in the fort, which also had a line of trenches outside, while Foster had a breastwork made of fence posts built around the fort. The next day, although they lacked any form of artillery, Foster's men maintained brisk musket fire on the American position, and Butterfield capitulated with 390 men and the cannons. Other skirmishes followed; the Americans retreated south and General Carleton's troops reoccupied Montreal, Chambly, and Saint-Jean.

Nova Scotia

A lesser-known invasion attempt was aimed at Nova Scotia. In the fall of 1776, Jonathan Eddy led a party of about 200 American volunteers seeking to invade Nova Scotia in the hope that a substantial part of its population would join the Americans. This would take place by crossing the Isthmus of Chignecto that unites the mainland of Nova Scotia with what was then the northern boundary of Massachusetts. However, Fort Cumberland guarded the isthmus. The five-point earth and stone star fort, which had been built by the French as Fort Beauséjour, was captured and renamed Cumberland by the British in 1755; by 1776, it was run down, having been previously vacant for eight years. The fort was reoccupied in June that year by a detachment of the Royal Fencible Americans, a Loyalist unit led by Colonel Joseph Goreham, and repairs to the fortifications and barracks were carried out. From November 10, 1776, the Americans surrounded Fort

Cumberland, but its loyal garrison would not surrender and it was besieged until November 29. That day, a British relief force landed nearby while Goreham and his men made a sortie from the fort; the Americans hastily retreated and Nova Scotia was secure for the rest of the war.

Most fortifications in Nova Scotia were located in the main settlement of Halifax, which was one of the Royal Navy's most important bases in North America due to its strategic location. During the war, the existing fortifications built since 1749 were strengthened. The earth and timber citadel on the hill dominating the town was enlarged to an irregular, elongated polygon plan measuring about 1,300ft long by 430ft wide. It was armed with up to 100 guns, and its highest part was crowned with a square redoubt enclosing an octagonal blockhouse. It was further surrounded by a ditch and pointed stakes. There were also several large batteries that covered the harbor's entrance.

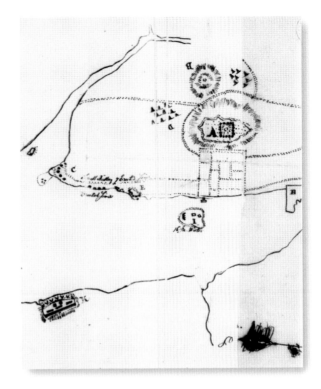

Halifax harbor fortifications, 1780. The citadel with its square redoubt is at the upper center; batteries are on the south side (left and center) and the town is enclosed in a square palisade. (Courtesy Library of Congress, Washington)

Hudson's Bay

An unusual raid took place on Hudson's Bay, northern Canada, in 1782. The first target was Fort Prince of Wales, a masonry bastioned work built since 1731 by the fur-trading monopoly Hudson's Bay Company, mounted with 42 cannons. During the 1690s, the French had raided and taken many trade forts, and this fort, located at the mouth of the Churchill River, was meant to be their protective citadel. On May 31, 1782, *Le Sceptre*, a 74-gun ship of the line, with two 36-gun frigates under the command of Jean-François de Galaup, comte de Lapérouse, who was destined to become one of the great

Fort Prince of Wales, Hudson's Bay, Canada. This masonry fort is truly extraordinary due to its location at Churchill (Manitoba) on the shores of Hudson's Bay facing the Arctic Ocean. Built laboriously from 1731 by the Hudson's Bay Company, it surrendered to Captain Lapérouse's French naval squadron in 1782. (Courtesy National Historic Sites, Parks Canada)

explorers of the South Pacific, sailed from Haiti. On board were 250 infantrymen and 40 gunners. On August 8, the squadron reached Fort Prince of Wales. The French troops landed and the bemused fur traders surrendered the fort (without a regular garrison) at the first summons. Lapérouse then sailed for forts York Factory and Severn, which also surrendered without a fight. All the forts were blown up and the French returned to Haiti. The economic damage was such that the company could not pay dividends for two years thereafter.

THE SOUTH

The first siege of Charleston, 1776

The British government had instructed its forces in America to occupy the southern colonies of Virginia, North and South Carolina, and Georgia so as to bolster the loyal portions of their population against their rebel neighbors. On June 1, 1776, a British fleet including 11 warships with 3,000 troops aboard was in sight off Charleston, South Carolina, with the purpose of occupying the South's most important city and harbor. This expeditionary force was under the command of Admiral Sir Peter Parker, whose flagship was the 50-gun HMS *Bristol*; General Clinton commanded the troops. Charleston was, however, a strongly patriot city and since March, anticipating a British intervention, its authorities had bolstered the city's defenses by building various entrenchments mounted with about 100 cannons. Most efforts went into building a large square fort with bastioned corners on Sullivan's Island to block ships going into Charleston's harbor.

Once anchored off Sullivan's Island, the British commanders spent nearly three weeks debating how to attack the fort. At length, the British troops under Clinton landed on marshy ground on Long Island. They were expected to cross a shallow sandbank at low tide onto the north end of Sullivan's Island, overrun a small redoubt with two guns, and take the fort at bayonet point. Meanwhile the fleet would quickly shatter the walls of the fort. On June 28, the ships moved towards the fort. The American gunners held their fire until the warships were at point blank range, then opened very effective fire. The Royal Navy return bombardment was also very intensive, but both sides realized that this fort was robust and remained hardly damaged. It was built of "palmetto logs and filled in with earth, our merlons were 16 feet thick, and high enough to cover the men from the fire of the tops," recalled Colonel William Moultrie, its commander. He further added that its "gate-way, (our gate not being finished) was barricaded with pieces of timber 8 or 10 inches square, which required

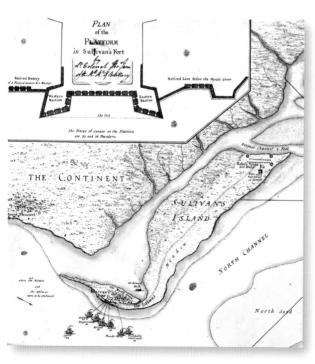

Detail from "A Plan of the attack on Fort Sullivan, near Charles Town in South Carolina by a squadron of His Majesty's ships" on June 28, 1776 – a print after Thomas James. At top is a plan of the face of the fort with its "Retired Battery" extensions on each side. At bottom is an area map showing the fort and the attacking ships. (Courtesy Library of Congress, Washington)

3 or 4 men to remove each piece." The softwood logs of local palmetto trees were placed in parallel lines, as in the classic construction of earth and timber walls, and they filled the 15¾ft space between with sand. As it turned out, the resilience of palmetto wood made it much better than hardwood for resisting artillery fire, the energy of the cannonballs being absorbed by its spongy nature. Another positive factor for the Americans was the tenacity and coolness of the 1,200 defenders and the highly professional artillery service they performed due to previous intensive training by two master gunners. On the British side, when the troops came to cross at low tide from the marshes, they were already much harassed by mosquitoes and now found that some of the passage was up to 7ft underwater; their assault was thus cancelled. The battle became solely an artillery duel and the ships were mercilessly raked, Admiral Parker's flagship being severely damaged. After a duel lasting nine hours and forty minutes, the British ships withdrew. The frigate HMS *Actaeon* ran into a sandbank and was burned by its crew to avoid capture. The overall American commander, Major-General Charles Lee, had meanwhile mobilized thousands of patriot militiamen and pressed all hands to build field fortifications around the city which now contained about 5,000 defenders. Even if Fort Sullivan (also called Moultrie) had fallen, it was unlikely the British could have taken Charleston. In the event, the attacking force suffered 205 men killed and wounded while the Americans had 37 men killed and wounded. It was another American triumph, in good part due to the rebels' remarkable talent for building good field fortifications and defending them courageously.

Inside the American fortifications on Sullivan's Island, Charleston, June 28, 1776 – a print after H. Charles McBarron. During the British fleet's bombardment, Sergeant William Jasper recovered the South Carolina flag that had been shot down and planted it on the parapet under intense artillery fire. His heroism greatly encouraged the American defenders in the partially completed palmetto log and sand fort on Sullivan's Island. (Courtesy US Army Center of Military History, Washington)

Savannah

Following France's entry into the war in mid-1778, Great Britain discovered that the newly reorganized and expanded French Navy was a transformed and efficient force that had little in common with the moribund fleet seen 20 years earlier. It now challenged, often successfully, the Royal Navy's command of the sea in the West Indies, where British islands were falling to French sea and land forces. The Americans had not benefited much from the alliance, apart from seeing the occasional French squadron off their coast, such as Admiral Charles Hector, comte d'Estaing's fleet's short appearance off Newport (Rhode Island) in August 1778. Meanwhile, the southern states were becoming the main theater of the war. Savannah had fallen to the British at the end of 1778 and the American forces under General Benjamin Lincoln were hard-pressed. The following year, he asked for French assistance; the British fleet was on the defensive and d'Estaing's fleet of 37 ships bearing 4,000 soldiers appeared off Savannah. It landed the troops on September 12, 1779; they were joined by Lincoln's 2,500 men on September 16. General Augustine Prévost, who commanded Savannah's 2,400-strong British garrison, spurned d'Estaing's summons to surrender five days later, and siege operations began. The French built trenches and batteries to the southeast.

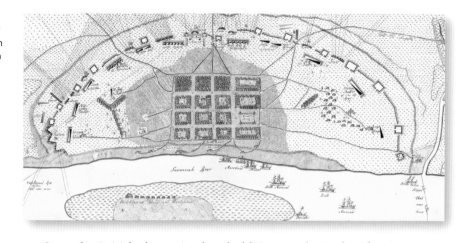

The fortifications around Savannah, August–September 1779, a detail from a larger pen and ink British map. The British Army built 15 redoubts and 13 batteries as well as many field fortifications along a crescent-shaped line that enclosed the city. (Courtesy Library of Congress, Washington)

Once the British determined to hold Savannah, its fortifications were greatly augmented in record time under the direction of engineer Captain James Moncrieff; a line of entrenchments with intervening redoubts was completed that now mounted about a hundred pieces of ordnance thanks to the unremitting labor of the troops as well as part of the town's residents. It is said that the French engineers building their own siege trenches were impressed by the speed in which the English engineers made "batteries spring like mushrooms," according to Porter's engineering history. There were 15 redoubts and 11 batteries, large and small, with earth entrenchments in between, laid out in a wide arc around the city, in front of which was an outer line of abatis overlooking swampy ground. The French and American troops found the marshy ground difficult for building siege works. Parallel trenches were only completed on September 23 and Prévost caused much havoc when some of his troops made a sortie the following day. Work pressed on, however, and by October 3 the siege batteries opened fire. The unforeseen length of the operations increasingly worried d'Estaing: even though the threat of the Royal Navy intervening was receding, the hurricane season was approaching. On October 9, a Franco-American assault against two redoubts was repulsed with heavy losses, d'Estaing being among some 600 wounded; over 200 were killed in the assault party. The siege was raised nine days later; the French fleet sailed away, while Lincoln went

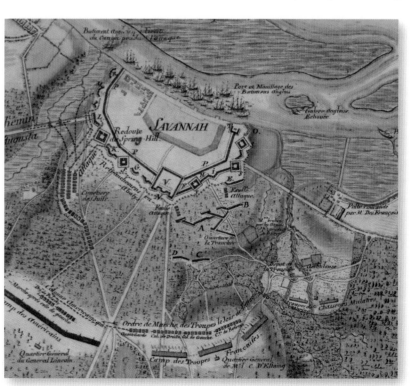

The siege of Savannah, Georgia, August–September 1779 – a detail from a larger French map by Pierre Ozanne. (Courtesy Library of Congress, Washington)

The fortifications at Savannah, 1782 – a detail from a larger American map. (Courtesy Library of Congress, Washington)

to Charleston. Prévost had conducted a brilliant defense, making maximum use of the fortifications so hastily built around Savannah. In 1780 a curtain wall with small bastions was built to enclose the city and a small citadel, named Fort Prévost, was erected at its eastern end.

The second siege of Charleston, 1780

Emboldened by success, an 8,500-strong British force under Sir Henry Clinton arrived from New York to launch an overland attack on the city of Charleston, which was defended by General Lincoln's 5,400 men. A further 5,000 British troops joined Clinton's army. Siege operations began on March 29 and were carried out efficiently in the classic textbook manner. The British built small redoubts, establishing the first parallel from April 1; the second parallel was finished on the 19th and the third parallel completed on May 6. American defense works built across the northern portion of the Charleston peninsula consisted of a large masonry redoubt (or hornwork)

Charleston, South Carolina, 1780, in a detail from a contemporary map. This map shows the fortifications built to protect the city on its northern and eastern flanks. The older fortification lined the city's shores on the Cooper and Ashley rivers. The defender's citadel was a large redoubt built in the middle of the northern line (marked "O") that was "picketed and raised, covered by Trous de Lous, double Abates, a canal from [the] Ashley to Cooper's River, and Batteries mounting 66 guns exclusive of mortars." (Courtesy, Library of Congress, Washington)

made "to form a Citadel with strong Lines and Redoubts [on both of its sides], picketed and raised, covered by Trous de Loup, double Abbatis, a canal from Ashley to Cooper River, and Batteries mounting 66 Guns exclusive of Mortars," according to the *Sketch of the Operations at Charleston*. Although these sounded formidable, the British drained the canal in early May by means of a sap and American senior officers knew that the works were, in fact, inadequate against such a strong force. The city surrendered on May 12. It was a serious blow to the Americans since the British now controlled the South's main cities.

Ninety Six

Patriot resistance went on in rural areas with troops in constant movement in the interior of the Carolinas. The occasional field fortification was built and abandoned as troops moved on, but there were exceptions

to this pattern. The most notable was the small village of Ninety Six occupying a strategic location in northwestern South Carolina. British Loyalist troops built fortifications there from December 1780, turning it into a stronghold. A stockade protected the village with a small redoubt at one end, but what made Ninety Six particularly strong was its unusual, eight-point star-shaped earthen redoubt erected by engineer Lieutenant Henry Haldane. Its walls were 14ft high and its ordnance consisted of three light 3pdr field pieces. The stockaded village and both redoubts were surrounded by an outer ditch and abatis. The star fort also had fraises protruding from its curtain walls.

By the spring of 1781, the Americans were winning in the South. After victories at Cowpens and Guilford Court House, General Greene with 1,000 men chose to attack Ninety Six, which had a garrison of 550 Loyalist troops led by Lieutenant-Colonel John Cruger. The star fort was its small citadel and it required a regular siege that began on May 22; under the direction of engineer Kosciuszko, trenches and parallels were dug and work also started on digging an underground mineshaft to blow up part of the curtain wall. A wooden tower about 30ft tall was also built for American marksmen to take out defenders on the walls. Cruger added sandbags on top raising the walls to 17ft that also gave good cover to Loyalist sharpshooters. Learning that a strong British relief force was approaching, Greene decided to storm both redoubts. At noon on June 18, a first assault group quickly overcame the smaller redoubt while a 50-man American "forlorn hope" rushed under fire into the ditch and started up the wall of the star fort. The latter were attacked by a sortie of 60 Loyalist soldiers, and retreated after desperate hand-to-hand fighting for the loss of 30 dead. The main attack had failed and the Americans also retreated from the small redoubt. Seeing this, Greene withdrew from Ninety Six before the British relief force arrived. The Americans had taken 150 casualties and the Loyalists nearly 100 during the siege. Ironically, Lord Rawdon, commander of the relief force, evacuated Ninety Six since its strategic value had become minimal due to operations elsewhere.

D SPANISH BATTERY, PENSACOLA, MAY 8, 1781

From March to May 1781, the Spanish forces besieging the British fortifications at Pensacola became more numerous as reinforcements arrived from the West Indies. By late April, the Spanish were applying standard siege procedures as they approached the powerful Queen's Redoubt, which was the key to the British defenses. Although considerably outnumbered, the British put up a stubborn defense that included a successful raid on the Spanish advanced works. Nevertheless, by early May the Spanish were methodically moving closer and building trenches and a redoubt as well as batteries for 24pdr heavy guns to pound the British works.

On June 6, two howitzers were mounted in the redoubt; the cannonade between the opponents was intense for the next two days, but, by the afternoon of May 7, a Spanish forward battery was started and was nearly completed by five in the morning of the 8th. An hour later, the British opened fire, "to which we replied with two howitzers from the redoubts," wrote General Gálvez, "with such success, that one of our grenades [howitzer shells] having fired the [British] powder magazine it

blew up the crescent [the Queen's Redoubt] with 105 men of the garrison." Francisco de Miranda, then a young officer who would later become a liberator of Venezuela, recalled vividly that "we heard a great explosion … and we saw a great column of smoke rising towards the clouds."

In terms of construction of siege works, Spanish engineers followed the same methods as their French allies and British opponents. The artillery they used was, however, of the older 1743 calibers and patterns since the Spanish version of the French Gribeauval system was brought into service after the war. Howitzer calibers were 7in. and 9in. At Pensacola, gun carriages would have been much as they had been since the 1740s. Their wood was often oil-stained although they could, at the time of the siege, also be painted red, grey, or black. The ironwork was black. Howitzers were of brass and featured a somewhat elongated breech. Spanish artillerymen were uniformed in dark blue with red collar and cuffs edged with yellow or gold lace, gold buttons, and gold-laced hats with red cockades.

West Florida

At the time of the American Revolution, Great Britain ruled over East Florida (with its powerful stone fort at St Augustine) and West Florida, which stretched from Pensacola to the eastern shore of the Mississippi River. Fort Condé, built with bricks and tabby (an oyster-shell concrete) by the French at Mobile, was the most extensive fort in West Florida; it was renamed Fort Charlotte in honor of Queen Charlotte of Mecklenburg-Strelitz, the wife of King George III. Fort Charlotte was not considered an important post by the British and was in some disrepair (see Fortress 49: *The Spanish Main 1492–1800* and Fortress 93: *The Forts of New France*). Other more remote places, such as Natchez, had relatively modest works consisting of simple stockaded enclosures or redoubts. For instance, the "field redoubt" near Baton Rouge named Fort New Richmond was described by the Spanish as "well fortified, with a ditch eighteen feet wide and nine deep; walls high and sloping, encompassed by a parapet adorned with chevaux-de-frise, crowned with 13 cannons of a large caliber" (*Gazetta de Madrid*, January 14, 1780). For its part, the enormous but largely unsettled part of French Louisiana west of the Mississippi River had been ceded to Spain during the 1760s along with its capital, New Orleans, which had modest earth fortifications around it.

Following Spain's declaration of war against Great Britain on May 8, 1779, Bernardo de Gálvez, the aggressive governor of Spanish Louisiana, led some 1,400 men, most of whom were militiamen, against British posts and quickly took the stockaded Fort Bute at Bayou Manchac, the field redoubt at Baton Rouge, and occupied Natchez in September 1779, thus eliminating enemy presence in the lower Mississippi Valley. Obtaining some reinforcements from Cuba, Gálvez next appeared off Mobile at the end of February 1780 with about 1,300 men. Mobile at this time was garrisoned by about 300 British regulars and militiamen. By March 12, the Spanish had invested Fort Charlotte and their completed siege batteries opened fire; their heavy guns soon made several breaches in the old walls and Mobile capitulated two days later.

Much further north at St Louis, a mixed force of between 750 and 1,500 British and Canadian fur traders and First Nations warriors attacked the town on May 26, 1780. Its defences consisted of a single stone tower 30ft in diameter and about 35ft high, with trenches between the tower and the river to the north and south of St Louis. The defences proved sufficient for a 29-man detachment of the Spanish Luisiana Regiment with about 180 militiamen to repel the attack. A simultaneous assault on nearby Cahokia was also repulsed by American troops led by George Rogers Clark. On January 12, 1781, a mixed Spanish-led force of Illinois volunteers and First Nations warriors took stockaded Fort St Joseph (at Niles, Michigan) by surprise and looted it before returning to St Louis.

Pensacola

Pensacola, the capital of British West Florida, was the only major British post left on the Gulf Coast. Founded by the Spanish at the end of the 17th century, it had been occupied by the British from 1763. They first built a naval yard and replaced the crumbling Spanish fort with a "Garrison Area" that featured a large stockade with blockhouses, a redoubt nearby on the north side, and a ditch on the seaward side. The senior commanders in Pensacola knew the town's few fortifications would be wholly inadequate against a powerful enemy force. A stronghold was needed and, during the 1770s Fort George

– a large square redoubt with half-bastions and armed with 20 cannons – was built on the lower part of Gage Hill, about 1,200 yards north of the town. Fort George featured an elongated hornwork that extended some 600ft southwest, and it was sited so as to cover the town of Pensacola further south; a large work named the Queen's Redoubt armed with 12 guns was erected on top of Gage Hill, so as to provide advance protection to Fort George from the north; another smaller fort, called the Prince of Wales Redoubt, was later constructed between Fort George and the Queen's Redoubt to protect communications. The harbor's entrance was guarded by Fort Barrancas Colorados (or Red Cliffs) armed with 11 guns. These works were made mainly of earth and brick since timber was scarce in Pensacola. Such as they were, these works provided Pensacola with a small citadel that might intimidate a modest hostile force, but was not likely to impress a numerous enemy army. Hopes for obtaining reinforcements from the British West Indies or from elsewhere in British North America were very slim and the Royal Navy was hard-pressed by the French and Spanish navies so that it no longer enjoyed naval supremacy in America.

On March 9, 1781, a Spanish fleet landed some 1,300 troops from Louisiana near Pensacola. Gálvez was again in command of the Spanish forces. There were some 1,300 British defenders under the command

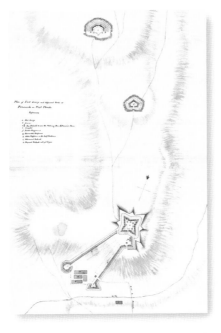

The forts at Pensacola, West Florida, c.1780–81. At top is the Queen's Redoubt, in the middle the Prince of Wales Redoubt, and below is Fort George, Pensacola's command center for British West Florida. The latter featured an extended hornwork to the south. (Courtesy, Library of Congress, Washington)

The capture of Pensacola, May 9, 1781. This print, after Lausan, was published in Paris after the war and seems to be based mainly on text descriptions. The works shown are liberal interpretations of written accounts, showing the explosion of the powder magazine. Troops wear French uniforms (with coat lapels, which the Spanish did not have) and General Gálvez (wearing a floppy hat) is certainly not taken from life, although his minor injury is shown by his left arm being in a sling. Although not dependable for detail, this work has artistic merit and appears to be the only near-contemporary illustration of the siege that has come to public attention. (Author's collection)

French troops marching towards Yorktown in October 1781, in a work signed "van Blarenberghe 1784." This is a composite view showing the abandoned British outworks in the foreground, the first and second parallel trench lines beyond, and the British works around Yorktown in the distance. (Courtesy Anne S. K. Brown Military Collection, Brown University Library, Providence, USA)

of Brigadier-General John Campbell in the three redoubts on the hill. Campbell knew this could only be the advance party of a much larger army and he resolved to put up as much resistance as possible. On March 18 and 19, the Fort Barrancas battery could not prevent Spanish ships led by Gálvez from entering the harbor, the indefensible town having been abandoned. During the following days and weeks, more regulars and militiamen arrived from Louisiana; everyone dug in, and opened siege operations in various parts of Gage Hill. They were joined on April 19 by a further 5,600 men from Havana and a detachment of over 700 French troops for a total of nearly 8,000 men. More scouting parties were sent out as the Spanish officers "had no exact plans, and the country was wooded," wrote Gálvez. From April 22, more trenches were opened, one coming to within 600 yards of the British fortifications, and a sizable earthen redoubt named Fort San Bernardo was built as well as other smaller ones. Batteries with heavy guns, notably 24pdrs, and mortars were also built to pound the first target: the Queen's Redoubt. By April 29, the Spanish had built long parallel trenches on each side of the British fortifications. There was constant artillery fire and frequent skirmishing. On May 4, at 12.30pm, the British "began a lively fire of mortars, cannons, and howitzers over the Queen's Redoubt," recalled Francisco de Miranda; meanwhile a party of about 200 soldiers made a sortie and took two Spanish advance redoubts, before destroying everything they could and withdrawing. As a result, the Spaniards reinforced their siege trenches and constructed a "wall of cotton bales and sand bags over the left wing of our [Spanish] parallel to cover the workers and to shelter the construction of the battery and cannons." For instance, Gálvez mentioned some "700 laborers with 300 fascines, sustained by 800 grenadiers and light infantry" working through the night of April 26/27.

Artillery duels also went on for days until May 8, when disaster overcame the British defenders. That morning, at 6.00am, the British opened fire from the Queen's Redoubt. The Spanish replied with two howitzers and, at 9.00am, a howitzer shell penetrated the powder magazine causing it to explode "with a terrifying noise," recalled Francisco Saavedra de Sangronis, killing 105 men. Spanish troops immediately rushed to occupy the badly damaged work and then turned its guns on Fort Prince of Wales; the latter's guns were soon overcome and it "fell silent." The garrison huddled in Fort George was now in a hopeless position and, on April 10, Campbell capitulated. The British lost 128 killed (including three officers) and 72 wounded. The Spanish suffered 94 killed (including ten officers) and 185 wounded. Although it had been a hard siege, and until the explosion occurred, the British had been well protected in their earth and timber redoubts while the Spanish attackers were in the classic siege situation of suffering higher casualties during the approach of their trenches. The casualties on both sides would likely have been much higher had there been an assault.

Although not immediately fully realized then, or later by some historians, the fall of Pensacola proved to be a tremendous blow to the British cause. Somewhat unexpectedly, Spain's land and naval forces achieved total control over the Mississippi Valley and the Gulf Coast turning the northern Caribbean Sea into a Spanish lake. There was no point in attacking what British forces remained at the fortress of St Augustine, in British East Florida, since that territory now had a very limited strategic importance to colonial powers. Furthermore, the fall of Pensacola was to be of huge importance to the future role of the United States as a continental power. Within the following 40 years, all the territories in the Mississippi Valley and the Gulf Coast were ceded to the United States; this was the far-flung result initiated by the capitulation of Pensacola.

Yorktown

In July 1780, a 6,000-strong French Army corps under General Jean-Baptiste Donatien de Vimeur, comte de Rochambeau arrived at Newport, Rhode Island, to act with the Continental Army under the supreme command of General Washington. This provided great encouragement to the Americans, and Washington was at first tempted to try to break the deadlock at New York; however, the idea came to nothing.

Meanwhile, the fighting in the Southern states took a turn for the better for the Americans from the beginning of 1781. Leaving Savannah and Charleston with British garrisons, General Cornwallis went to Yorktown, Virginia, arriving with his troops in late August. A new Franco-American plan emerged that called for a combined sea and land operation. Rochambeau's army would come out of Newport and join Washington's army outside

A model of Yorktown and the fortifications around it. In the foreground are the first parallel trenches with redoubts and batteries built from October 6, 1781, by the combined French and American Army. In the middle ground is the second parallel built from October 11–12 with, at right, numbers 9 and 10 redoubts incorporated in this line after their capture on October 14. At the center is the site of the surrender of General Cornwallis' sword on October 19. Near the top is Yorktown surrounded by British works. Sunken British ships can be seen in the York River. (Colonial National Historic Park, Yorktown; author's photograph)

of New York, and then the united force would march down to besiege Cornwallis in Yorktown; Admiral François de Grasse would come out of the West Indies with a powerful French fleet, land additional French troops to join the combined army, and keep Admiral Samuel Graves' British squadron cruising off Virginia at bay. The plan worked and, in early September de Grasse, enjoying naval superiority, compelled Graves to withdraw to New York. The British forces in Yorktown could not be withdrawn by sea and were surrounded by a combined army of some 22,600 men, 8,600 of whom were French.

Generals Rochambeau and Washington at the siege of Yorktown, October 1781, in a painting by Pierre Ganne after a work by Auguste Couder. As implied in this illustration, the technical aspects of the siege's works were largely left – with Washington's agreement – to the French Army, which had numerous and excellent staff and engineer officers, some of which are seen in this evocative canvas. General Lafayette is shown just behind Washington; a senior French engineer officer is at right pouring over a plan. (Colonial National Historic Park, Yorktown; author's photograph)

Yorktown was situated on a point of land projecting from the southern shore of the York River, which created a narrow passage in conjunction with Gloucester Point on the north shore of the river. Both sides were occupied by British troops. Soon after they arrived, the British troops set about building a line of earthworks featuring ten redoubts around Yorktown's landward side with an additional hornwork on the southwest flank that commanded the road to Hampton. Of the redoubts built, numbers 9 and 10 were outer works for additional strength built on slightly elevated ground south of the line of earthworks. Cornwallis was somewhat deficient of artillery and had to borrow guns from the few British warships in the river to arm the 14 batteries constructed along the line; they eventually mounted 65 cannons, but the highest calibre guns available were 18pdrs. A few outlying redoubts were built

E FRENCH MORTAR BATTERY, YORKTOWN, OCTOBER 1781

Mortars were arguably amongst the most dangerous pieces of ordnance to operate at that time. Bombardiers, the specialized gunners supervising mortar service, thus had higher pay and followed a precise procedure to minimize risks. Mortars were mostly used during sieges by both the defenders and the attackers. To load the mortar, in whose chamber a suitable powder charge had been inserted, it had to point straight up as shown here. A hollow, cast-iron spherical bomb filled with powder and debris with a fuse was then brought by two soldiers, hooked on a timber pole. The bomb was inserted into the mortar's chamber on top of the powder charge. The bomb's fuse was lit by a bombardier. The mortar was then aimed to its predetermined angle and fired by lighting its breech vent. If all went well, the bomb would fly in an arc trajectory and was timed to explode when falling close to its target.

At Yorktown, mortars were an important feature in the tactics of the allied army to subdue the town. A French plan shows that the second parallel, whose artillery fired at point blank range, included 16 mortars in two batteries. Probably all of Rochambeau's 12 mortars (of 8in. and 12in. caliber) were

mounted there. These were likely of the older Vallières pattern since the Gribeauval-pattern mortars were cast from 1785. The French mortars at Yorktown fired over 3,500 bombs during the siege. The allied army had great quantities of fascines, gabions, sandbags, and other items for erecting field fortifications as in Europe, as well as detailed building instruction for the troops.

The uniform of the Corps Royal de l'Artillerie (Royal Corps of Artillery) was then dark blue, including the coat's collars, shoulder straps and lapels, with red cuffs, lining, and piping, and trimmed with brass buttons. Bombardiers were distinguished by two yellow chevrons worn on the coat's lower left sleeve. The hat had black edging lace and the cockade was very likely the "alliance" type symbolizing white for France and black for the United States. For serving the guns, muskets and accoutrements were laid aside and some gunners might only have undress vests that were dark blue or white with red cuffs and forage caps. A "Roman" short sword was introduced for the men from 1775, but many probably still had the older model hanger with a "D" guard. Officers had the same uniform, but of better quality cloth and with gold buttons and epaulets.

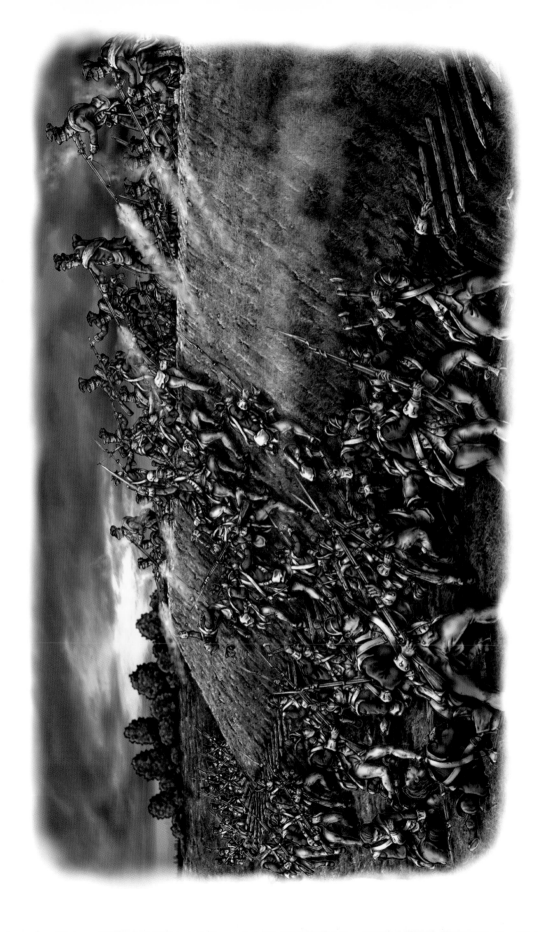

further away and a smaller line of earthworks with five redoubts also enclosed Gloucester Point.

In early October, the combined army arrived in the area. Gloucester Point was blockaded with field fortifications by Brigadier-General Claude de Choisy's corps consisting of Lauzun's Legion, half hussars and half infantry with 800 French marines and American troops. There was no intention of storming the point, but when Lieutenant-Colonel Banastre Tarleton with his British Legion cavalry did exit it on October 3, he was driven back in by the hussars led by Lauzun in person. The main army was meanwhile

The French attack on the British Redoubt No. 9 at Yorktown, evening of October 14, 1781, in a print after Jacques Onfroy de Bréville in F. Trevor Hill's *Washington, The Man of Action* (1914). At right is the Royal Deux-Ponts Regiment in sky-blue coats with an officer waving the regimental color; at left are the grenadiers of the Gatinois Regiment in white uniforms attacking with a cry of *"Vive le Roi!"* ("Long Live the King!") Fighting was intense and the 400 attackers suffered 15 killed and 77 wounded; the Hessians and British counted 18 killed and about 40–50 wounded and prisoners. (Author's collection)

occupying the outer redoubts abandoned by the British, setting up camps, moving up the siege artillery, and surveying the area outside of Yorktown on the west side of the river. It was agreed that the terrain was suitable for a siege involving parallel trenches with earthen siege batteries. The siege artillery used by Rochambeau's army consisted of 12 24pdrs and eight 16pdrs of the new artillery system introduced by Lieutenant-General Jean-Baptiste Vaquette de Gribeauval. It was the first deployment in battle of the Gribeauval system and proved to be very satisfactory. The four 8in. and eight 12in. French mortars were most likely of the older de Vallière design, still considered suitable for siege operations. The American artillery was more varied and numerous consisting of 27 18pdrs, three 24pdrs, ten 10in. mortars, two 8in. mortars and three 8in. howitzers for a total of 73 pieces of artillery for the allied army. On October 6, everything was ready and the building of the trenches by some 4,300 men for the first parallel started in the evening. By the morning of October 7, it was practically finished; this first line featured seven batteries and four redoubts, but it was only the preliminary work, which applied classic siege tactics as practiced in Europe on a scale rarely

F AMERICAN ASSAULT ON THE BRITISH REDOUBT NO. 10 AT YORKTOWN, EVENING OF OCTOBER 14, 1781

Earthen and wood redoubts, even as simple field fortifications, were very effective defense works that required great efforts to be overcome by the opposing force. Storming such a place could exact considerable sacrifice from an attacking force that, in spite of much heroism, might fail to take it. The classic assault force consisted of a forward party called the "forlorn hope" made up of elite soldiers, grenadiers, and light infantrymen with pioneers. The French Army called this party *les enfants perdus* (the lost children), which gives an idea of the survival rate expected. During the first years of the war, American troops were not trained in this type of action, but as time went by, they became more proficient in various aspects of European siege warfare as shown by the successful assaults of Stoney Point and Paulus Hook.

At Yorktown, 400 American light infantrymen under the command of Colonel Alexander Hamilton were tasked with assaulting Redoubt No. 10 held by 70 British soldiers while the French would assault Redoubt No. 9. On the evening of October 14, the assault parties attacked. The Americans silently surrounded their objective and moved up with unloaded muskets, so as to not alert the British, for a bayonet assault. This illustration shows what happened once they reached the ditch and struggled to climb up the parapet; pioneers hacked to cut away the row of pointed logs meant to hamper any attackers while those soldiers that got across the logs managed to fight their way into the redoubt. The British resisted fiercely with musketry fire and hand grenades, but the Americans quickly overcame them, losing only nine killed and 25 wounded – a remarkably low figure.

American troops storming and entering the No. 10 British Redoubt at Yorktown, October 14, 1781. This oil painting of the famous assault was made by renowned French artist Eugène-Louis Lami in 1840. It shows a remarkably good rendering of the redoubt's profile with hand-to-hand combat all around. (Courtesy Virginia State Capitol, Richmond)

seen in America. By October 9 and 10, the French and American siege batteries started bombarding the British positions in Yorktown with heavy artillery including 24pdr guns and siege mortars, which poured a multitude of projectiles onto the town and also towards the few British ships in its harbor. British artillerymen did what they could, but they were outgunned and, from that date, their response became slower and more sporadic.

During the night of October 11/12, the trenches for the second parallel, which was only 360 yards from the British positions, were dug by thousands of men to a depth of 3½ft and a width of 7ft. To complete the line of this new parallel, the British redoubts numbers 9 and 10 had to be captured. On October 14 at about 8.00pm, as dusk was setting in, six howitzers fired in quick succession gave the assault signal. No. 9 Redoubt, which was the largest and had a bastion shape, was attacked by 400 grenadiers and chasseurs of the Royal Deux-Ponts and Gatinois regiments while No. 10 Redoubt, which was smaller and square, was assaulted by elite battalions of American light infantry. The British and Hessian soldiers put up a fierce resistance, but, after half an hour of epic fighting, both redoubts were taken. They were then incorporated into the attackers' second parallel line, which was completed on October 17, bringing the British positions within point blank range of newly built French and American batteries. This put the defenders of Yorktown – which had already been under intense, round-the-clock bombardment for the past nine days – in a hopeless situation. Cornwallis and his officers knew it and asked for an armistice to discuss surrender terms. By then, the allies had fired some 15,437 rounds on the British positions, an average of a shot a minute round the clock since the start of the siege. On October 19, the British capitulated and a total of 8,091 surrendered. The allies had taken 389 casualties, the British and German troops perhaps as many as 904. It was the last major battle in North America, and from then on, it was obvious that Great Britain would lose the war.

THE MIDWEST

The territories in the western wilderness up to the eastern shore of the Upper Mississippi River had nominally belonged to Great Britain since the 1763

A French plan of the siege of Yorktown shown shortly before its capitulation on October 19, 1781, from *Plan figuré a vue du siège d'York*. Following their October 14 capture of British redoubts 9 and 10, the French and Americans incorporated them into their second parallel, which poured grueling fire from its batteries close to the British fortifications. The now-abandoned first parallel can be seen beneath it. The French positions are indicated in yellow, American in green, and British in red. (Courtesy Archives Nationales [France], Outremer, Dépot des Fortifications des Colonies, Amérique septentrionale, 03DFC0009B02)

Treaty of Paris. In 1778, a small group of American riflemen led by George Rogers Clark left Virginia and floated west down the Ohio River to "the Illinois Country" on the east shore of the Mississippi. The first objective was to take the old fort on a cliff above Kaskaskia, which was easily done by a surprise attack on July 4 in which there were no casualties; nearby Cahokia also capitulated. The local inhabitants were of French origin and quite happy to learn from Clark of France's alliance with the United States; some joined his force. The next target was Fort Sackville at Vincennes (Indiana) on the Wabash River, whose strategic position controlled much territory for the British between the Great Lakes and the Mississippi. After a grueling march, Clark and about 170 men arrived in the vicinity of Vincennes in late February 1779.

Vincennes

The first fort at Vincennes was built by the French in 1732, but had vanished by the 1770s. The place was defenseless when British Lieutenant Governor Edward Abbott arrived there in April 1777; worried about marauding First Nations warriors, Abbott decided to build a stockade fort as well as organize the inhabitants into three companies of militia. Named after the British politician Lord George Germain who had been known as Lord Sackville until 1770, Fort Sackville was built near the Wabash River during the summer and fall of 1777. The stockade was quadrangular in shape with its four sides having different lengths. The west wall was 215ft in length. The north side was 190ft long and contained a gate. The south wall was 165ft and the east side was 203ft long. The logs of the stockade walls were leveled at 11ft high. Midway along each wall was a salient angle with firing platforms inside. Abbott's two-story headquarters building was located in the northeast part of the fort. It was not a formidable fort, but could keep warriors out. Abbott's successor, Lieutenant Governor Henry Hamilton, arrived in December 1778

CONSTRUCTION OF A STOCKADE

The quickest and most common way to put up a fortification was to erect a stockade (also called palisade) wall made of logs, especially in the wilder frontier regions. In North America, trees to make logs were readily available near most fort sites; once cut down and pared of branches, they would be made to a uniform length that, on average, would be from 12ft to 16ft high and about 1ft in diameter. The top end of the log was pointed. A narrow trench of about 4ft to 5ft in depth outlining the fort's perimeter was dug and the logs, points up, were set in one

against the other. The upper part was secured together by narrower squared timbers nailed in and firing ports hewed out between logs at regular intervals; larger ports for cannons could also be pierced. Banquettes or firing steps of packed earth or wooden boards lined the base of the stockade in the fort's interior. Stockades were also often built as outer obstacles of large earth and timber fortifications and were also occasionally to be found, but somewhat shorter at about 6ft to 8ft in height, as berms in the middle of the ditches outside these large works.

with a detachment of approximately 40 regular British soldiers and was immediately unimpressed by the fort, which he resolved to strengthen.

Hamilton's original concept called for a blockhouse over each corner, but this does not seem to have been done. At the suggestion of Major Jehu Hay, his second in command, two blockhouses of squared logs were built on top of opposite corners of the stockade at the northeast and southwest angles. Their two salient angles were corrected to straight walls, as were those at two other corners later on. It is known that the southwest blockhouse was musketproof, and had two levels, the lower with firing slots for muskets and the upper with five gun ports for a 3pdr cannon; the other blockhouse was probably identical. A powder magazine, a well, and a second barrack building 40ft long by 18ft wide were built inside and the parade ground covered with gravel. All of the above is from documentary and archaeological evidence (conducted by Indiana University from 1969 to 1971), but many aspects remain debatable and it is not always clear if the remains are of Fort Sackville since the earlier French fort and a later American fort built in 1812 occupied the same area. Thus, the exact location of the fort is not known. What is known is that its northwest blockhouse was completed on February 22, 1779. The next day, George Rogers Clark's American force attacked and, after a short fight, the fort surrendered on February 24. As a result of Clark's successful campaign, the British eventually ceded to the United States a vast area that includes the present states of Ohio, Indiana, Illinois, Michigan, Wisconsin, and the eastern portion of Minnesota.

THE SITES TODAY

The reader will not be too surprised to note that many of the original fortifications mentioned in this study have largely vanished. This is mostly due to the effects of erosion and rot on earth and wooden structures over time, as well as dramatic development and large-scale urbanization in the

The British evacuate Fort Sackville at Vincennes, February 25, 1779. American commander George Rogers Clark salutes British Colonel Henry Hamilton marching out of the fort with his garrison between lines of American riflemen. The fort's garrison had surrendered the previous day after a brief fight. This print, after H. Charles McBarron, shows three blockhouses of the five blockhouses it was initially believed to have, but further research and archaeological surveys by Indiana University indicate there may have been only two, although Colonel Hamilton originally planned to have four. The top level of the blockhouses had gun ports as well as musket loops. (Courtesy US Army Center of Military History, Washington)

The remains of No. 10 Redoubt at the Colonial National Historic Park, Yorktown. Part of it has collapsed into the York River due to erosion and trees have grown tall over what used to be a fairly clear field of fire two-and-a-half centuries ago. Some restoration was done with pickets added during the 20th century. Captain Stephen Olney, leading the mostly African-American light infantry company of the Rhode Island Regiment on October 14, 1781, later recalled that the assault column approached the redoubt "in silence, with guns unloaded, and in good order. Many, no doubt, thinking that less than one quarter of a mile would finish the journey of life." The 400 Americans who triumphed on that site were fortunate in having only nine killed and 25 wounded. (Author's collection)

United States and Canada since 1783. There are, however, some very worthy surviving sites that can be visited. Possibly the most extensive, which is certain to be a delight to anyone interested in fortifications, is Quebec City. It has had many changes since 1775, including the addition of a mighty citadel since the 1830s; its preserved masonry fortifications make it the only major walled fortress city in North America and visitors will find site markers to events of 1775–76. At Fort Beauséjour National Historic Site (the former Fort Cumberland), the events of the 1776 siege are evoked by the still substantial grass-covered earth and stone curtain walls and displays. In terms of siege works, the Yorktown battlefield gives an excellent sense of this type of fortification in a grand setting encompassing the distances between the besiegers and the besieged.

Little remains of Pensacola's fortifications, which have been built over, apart from a modest reconstruction of a small slice of Fort George's brick and earth wall at the corner of Palafox and Jackson streets. Bunker Hill Monument has a very high obelisk monument, but almost all the original features of the 1775–76 siege of Boston have long been built over. For the many earth and timber fortifications erected during the war, the fine reconstruction of Fort Stanwyx National Monument (in Rome, NY) is a must to visualize this type of work; it is situated in a lovely area.

For more information, the reader might enjoy consulting the American National Register of Historic Places (http://www.nps.gov/nr) and the Canadian Register of Historic Places (http://www.pc.gc.ca/progs/rclp-crhp). In closing, we laud the United States National Park Service that admirably fulfils its mandate by allowing free (or minimally charged for specific services) access to anyone visiting sites such as Fort Stanwix, Saratoga, and many others since they "belong to the American people" who pay for their upkeep through their taxes, thus allowing ordinary young families to experience the nation's vast heritage. This is also true for the US national and many of its state museums. Sadly, that excellent and respectful attitude towards the taxpaying public is not followed by Parks Canada historic sites and Canada's national and provincial museums.

BIBLIOGRAPHY

Blanchard, Anne, *Les Ingénieurs du "Roy" de Louis XIV à Louis XVI*, Université Paul Valéry: Montpelier (1979)

— —, *Dictionnaire des ingénieurs militaires*, Université Paul Valéry: Montpelier (1981)

Bolton, Reginald Pelham, *Relics of the Revolution*, (np) New York (1916)

Bonner, William Thompson, *New York: The World's Metropolis*, R. L. Polk & Co.: New York (1924)

Castonguay, Jacques, *Les défis du fort Saint-Jean*, Les édition du Richelieu: Saint-Jean (1975)

Fireman, Janet R., *The Spanish Royal Corps of Engineers in the Western Borderlands: Instrument of Bourbon Reform 1764 to 1815*, The Arthur H. Clark Company: Glendale, CA (1977)

Fiske, John, *The American Revolution*, 2 Vols, (np) Boston (1898)

Fuss, Norman, "The British Corps of Engineers in America 1775–1783," *Military Collector & Historian: Journal of the Company of Military Historians*, 66:4 (Winter 2014) and 67:1 (Spring 2015)

Galgano, Francis A., "Revolutionary War in the Hudson Highlands: Fortifying West Point 1775–1779," *Middle States Geographer*, 43 (2010)

Gálvez, Bernardo de, "Diary of the operations against Pensacola," *Louisiana Historical Quarterly*, I:1 (January 1917)

Greene, Jerome A., *The Guns of Independence: The Siege of Yorktown 1781*, El Dorado Hills, CA: Savas Beatie (2005) [Author's note: readers wishing to find out more about the latest archaeological findings and other structural details should consult this excellent work.]

Haarmann, Albert W., "The Spanish Conquest of British West Florida 1779–1781," *Florida Historical Quarterly*, XXXIX: 2 (October 1960)

Holmes, Jack D. L., *Honor and Fidelity*, (np) Birmingham, AL (1965)

Johnston, Henry P., *The Yorktown Campaign and the Surrender of Cornwallis*, Harper: New York (1881)

Miranda, Francisco de, "Miranda's Diary of the Siege of Pensacola," Donald E. Worcester (ed.), *Florida Historical Quarterly*, XXIX: 3 (January 1951)

Porter, Whitworth, *History of the Corps of Royal Engineers*, Vol. I, (np) London (1896)

Quesada, Alejandro de, *A History of Florida's Forts*, The History Press: Charleston, SC (2006)

Rea, Robert R., "Pensacola under the British 1763–1781," in McGovern, James (ed.), *Colonial Pensacola*, University of West Florida: Pensacola (1974)

Saavedra de Sangronis, Francisco de, *The Journal of Don Francisco Saavedra de Sangronis 1780–1783*, Pardon, Francisco Morales (ed.) and Topping, Aileen Moore (trans.), University of Florida Press: Gainesville (1989)

Sanguinet, M., *L'invasion du Canada par les Bastonois – Journal de M. Sanguinet*, Ministère des affaires culturelles: Quebec (1975)

Smith, George, *A Universal Military Dictionary*, (np) London (1779)

Stanley, George, *Canada Invaded 1775–1776*, Hakkert: Toronto (1973)

Walker, Paul K., *Engineers of Independence: A Documentary History of the Army Engineers in the American Revolution 1775–1783*, Office of History, US Army Corps of Engineers: Washington (1981). [Author's note: many quotations in our study are taken from this fine compilation.]

Wilson, James Grant, *The Memorial History of the City of New York*, Vol. 2, New York History Company: New York (1892)

Winsor, Justin (ed.), *Narrative and Critical History of America*, Vol. VI, Boston
    (1887)
Wright, Robert K., *The Continental Army*, US Army Center of Military History:
    Washington (1989)
Young, Richard J., "Blockhouses 1749–1841: A Comparative Report and
    Catalogue," *Canadian Historic Sites Occasional Papers in Archaeology
    and History*, 23, Parks Canada: Ottawa (1980)

GLOSSARY

Abbatis	A defensive barricade or row of obstructions made up of closely spaced felled trees, their tops toward the enemy, their branches trimmed to points and interlaced where possible.
Banquette	A continuous step or ledge at the interior base of a parapet on which defenders stood to direct musket fire over the top of the wall. A fire step.
Bastion	A projection of the curtain wall, usually at the corners, made up of four sides, two faces and two flanks, which better enabled a garrison to defend the ground adjacent with crossfire.
Battery	An emplacement for artillery.
Berm	A line of wooden stakes or logs, 6ft–8ft long, planted in the middle of a ditch and pointing vertically.
Breastwork	See *Parapet*.
Casemate	A mortar-proof or shellproof chamber located within the walls of defensive works; generally pierced with openings for weapons, loopholes for muskets, or embrasures for cannon.
Chandelier	A movable parapet placed over the ground, made of wooden frames, on which fascines or other filling material were laid.
Cordon	The coping or top course of a scarp or a rampart, sometimes of different coloured stone and set proud from the rest of the wall. The point where a rampart stops and a parapet begins.
Counterguard	A defensive work built in a ditch in front of a bastion to give it better protection.
Counterscarp	The outer side of a ditch or moat. See also *Scarp*.
Covered way	A depression, road or path in the outer edge of a fort's moat or ditch, generally protected from enemy fire by a parapet, at the foot of which might be a banquette enabling the coverage of the glacis with musketry.
Cunette	A furrow located in the bottom of a dry ditch for the purpose of drainage.
Curtain	The wall of a fort between two bastions.
Demi-bastion	A half-bastion with only one face and one flank.
Demi-lune	A triangular-shaped defensive work built in a ditch in front of a bastion or a curtain wall. Also termed a *Ravelin*.

Ditch	A wide, deep trench around a defensive work. When filled with water, it was termed a moat or wet ditch; otherwise a dry ditch or fossé.
Embrasure	An opening in a wall or parapet allowing cannon to fire through it, the gunners remaining under cover. The sides of the embrasure were called cheeks, the bottom the sole, the narrow part of the opening the throat, and the wide part the splay.
En barbette	An arrangement for cannon to be fired directly over the top of a low wall instead of through embrasures.
Enfilade fire	Fire directed from the flank or side of a body of troops, or along the length of a ditch, parapet, or wall. Guns in the flank of a bastion can direct enfilade fire along the face of the curtain.
Epaulement	A parapet or work protecting against enfilade fire.
Fascines	Long bundles of sticks or small-diameter tree branches bound together for use in revetments, for stabilizing earthworks, filling ditches, etc.
Flèche	A field fortification work of two faces, usually raised.
Fossé or foss	See *Ditch (dry)*.
Fraise	A defense of closely placed stakes or logs, 6ft–8ft long, driven or dug into the ground and sharpened; arranged to point horizontally or obliquely outward from a defensive position.
Gabion	A large, round, woven wicker cylinder intended to be set in place and filled with earth, sand, or stones.
Gallery	An interior passageway or corridor that runs along the base of a fort's walls.
Gate	A main entrance of a fortress.
Glacis	A broad, gently sloped earthwork or natural slope in front of a fort, separated from the fort proper by a ditch and outworks and so arranged as to be swept with musket or cannon fire.
Gorge	The interval or space between the two curtain angles of a bastion. In a ravelin, the area formed by the flanked angle and either left open or enclosed.
Guardhouse	The headquarters for the daily guard.
Guérite	A small lookout watchtower, usually located on the upper outer corner of a bastion.
Half-bastion	See *Demi-bastion*.
Hornwork	A work made up of a bastion front, two half-bastions and a curtain, and two long sides termed branches.
Loopholes	Small openings in walls or stockades through which muskets are fired.
Machicoulis	Projections in old castles and over gates, left open above to throw stones etc. on enemies below.
Magazine	A place for the storage of gunpowder, arms, or goods generally related to ordnance.
Merlon	The solid feature between embrasures in a parapet.
Moat	See *Ditch*.
Orgue	See *Portcullis*.

Outwork	An outer defense, inside the glacis but outside of the body of the place. A ravelin is an outwork.
Palisade	A high fence made of stakes, poles, palings, or pickets, supported by rails and set endwise in the ground. See *Stockade*.
Parapet	A breastwork or protective wall over which defenders, standing on banquettes, fire their weapons.
Portcullis	A timber or iron grating that can be lowered to close the gates of a fortress.
Postern	A passage leading from the interior of a fortification to the ditch.
Rampart	The mass of earth, usually faced with masonry, formed to protect an enclosed area.
Ravelin	An outwork consisting of two faces forming a salient angle at the front and a flank angle to the rear that was usually closed at the gorge. Ravelins are separated from the main body of the place by ditches and function to protect curtains. Also called a *Demi-lune*.
Redoubt	An enclosed fortification without bastions.
Revetment	The sloping wall of stone or brick supporting the outer face of a rampart.
Sallyport	A passageway within the rampart, usually vaulted, leading from the interior of a fort to the exterior, primarily to provide for sorties.
Sap	A trench and parapet constructed by besiegers to protect their approaches toward a fortification.
Scarp	The interior side of a ditch or the outer slope of a rampart. See also *Counterscarp*.
Stockade	A line or enclosure of logs or stakes set upright in the earth with no separation between them, to form a barrier eight or more feet high. Stockades were generally provided with loopholes. The loopholes were reached by banquettes or elevated walks. See also *Palisade*.
Tabby	A cement-like building material made up of ground oyster shells, lime, and sand, mixed with salt water. Used especially in the southern colonies.
Traverse	A parapet or wall thrown across a covered way, a terreplein, a ditch, or other location to prevent enfilade or reverse fire along a work.
Trou de loup	A usually small pit in the form of an inverted cone, dug as an obstacle and having a pointed stake in the middle.

INDEX

Note: page numbers in **bold** refer to illustrations, captions and plates.